Financial Management

Essentials You Always Wanted To Know

VIBRANT
PUBLISHERS

Financial
Management
Essentials You Always Wanted To Know

ISBN-10: 1-946383-64-3
ISBN-13: 978-1-946383-64-8
Library of Congress Control Number: 2011911768

The publisher wishes to thank Kalpesh Ashar (India) for his valuable inputs to this edition.

Vibrant Publishers books are available at special quantity discount for sales promotions, or for use in corporate training programs. For more information please write to **bulkorders@vibrantpublishers.com**

Please email feedback / corrections (technical, grammatical or spelling) to **spellerrors@vibrantpublishers.com**

To access the complete catalogue of Vibrant Publishers, visit **www.vibrantpublishers.com**

Table of Contents

Dear Reader,

Thank you for purchasing **Financial Management Essentials You Always Wanted To Know.** We are committed to publishing books that are content-rich, concise and approachable enabling more readers to read and make the fullest use of them. We hope this book provides you the most enriching learning experience.

Should you have any questions or suggestions, feel free to email us at **reachus@vibrantpublishers.com**

Thanks again for your purchase.

- Vibrant Publishers Team

Books in
Self-Learning Management Series

**Cost Accounting and Management
Essentials You Always
Wanted To Know**
ISBN: 978-1-946383-62-4

**Financial Accounting
Essentials You Always
Wanted To Know**
ISBN: 978-1-946383-66-2

**Project Management
Essentials You Always
Wanted To Know**
ISBN: 978-1-946383-60-0

**Financial Management
Essentials You Always
Wanted To Know**
ISBN: 978-1-946383-64-8

For the most updated list of books visit
www.vibrantpublishers.com

facebook.com/vibrantpublishers

Chapter **1**

Introduction to Financial Management

Financial Management is a field of finance that deals with the use of financial information of a company to take decisions. The diagram below shows the steps in the analysis of financial information.

Financial Accounting is a field that deals with the preparation of financial statements (refer the book "Financial Accounting Essentials You Always Wanted to Know" of this series).

Financial Management uses this information to first analyze the company's health and then to take appropriate decisions.

Consider, for example, the Balance Sheet and Income Statement of two companies as below:

Balance Sheet (in million $)	ABC Inc.	XYZ Inc.
Current Assets		
Cash	$20	$10
Inventory	$50	$20
Total Current Assets	$70	$30
Long-term Assets		
Long-term investment	$230	$70
Property, plant & equipment (net)	$1,000	$800
Total Assets	$1,300	$900
Current Liabilities	$30	$5
Long-term Liabilities		
Long-term debt	$100	$40
Bonds	$500	$50
Total Liabilities	$630	$95
Stockholders' Equity		
Paid-in capital	$200	$300
Retained earnings	$470	$505
Total stockholders' equity	$670	$805
Total Liabilities & Equity	$1,300	$900

Income Statement (in million $)	ABC Inc.	XYZ Inc.
Sales revenues	$150	$100
Cost of Goods Sold	$100	$60
Gross Profit	$50	$40
Selling, general, and administrative expenses	$10	$8
Depreciation expense	$20	$15
Operating income (EBIT)	$20	$17
Interest expense	$5	$2
Profit before taxes (PBT)	$15	$15
Income tax expense	$3	$3
Net Income	$12	$12

From the above financial statements, it is evident that both the companies have the same Net Income ($12 million).Following questions arise:

a) As a banker, is this information enough to extend a loan to both the companies?

b) As an investor, does this mean goods returns?

c) As a manager, are these returns the best in the industry?

Just by looking at the individual numbers in the financial statements it is not possible to answer the above questions. In order to answer them one needs to do financial statement analysis that looks at a combination of numbers that provides more information. This analysis compares a combination of financial numbers (ratios) over a period of time for a company and also compares these with other companies in the same industry. This analysis is done using two tools given below:

a) Ratio analysis

b) Common-size financial statements

Using the data from the financial statement analysis companies make appropriate decisions to ensure that they meet their ultimate business objective – maximization of their stock price. The decisions are taken in the following areas:

a) Cost of Capital

b) Capital Budgeting

c) Working Capital Management

d) Capital Structure & Leverage

e) Dividend Policy

Finally, companies use Pro forma financial statement to do a what-if analysis and estimate their financial statements for the next period (quarter/year). Companies also use financial control systems to maintain control on their financial decisions.

The later chapters describe each of the above areas in detail, starting with the financial statement analysis, followed by financial decision making, and finally forecasting financial statements.

Chapter **2**

Financial Statement Analysis

Analysis of Financial Statements is done using financial ratios and common-size financial statements. In this chapter we shall discuss both techniques in detail.

Ratio Analysis

The financial statements of a company report the company's position at a given point in time (Balance Sheet) and its operations over a period of time (Income Statement and Statement of Cash Flows). This data can be used by the company's management, bankers and investors to predict future and to plan actions to improve it. But this analysis is more useful when done using financial ratios instead of individual numbers from the financial statements. For example, consider a company paying $100,000 interest on its debt of $1,000,000, and another company paying $50,000 interest on its debt of $700,000. If one needs to know which company is financially stronger then it is done by comparing the company's interest expense with respect to its debt, studying the company's debt with respect to its total assets, comparing the interest paid against the income of the company and comparing its debt structure with that of other firms in the same industry.

In order to do the above analysis, ratios are to be formed using data from the balance sheet, income statement and the statement of cash flows of the company. There are several ratios that exist and each has a different purpose. Some ratios involve only balance sheet items or income statement items or items from the statement of cash flows. Others involve a combination of items from these three statements. In the sections below we see how ratios are computed and used for decisions making with the help of financial statements of AllFresh food producing company:

Balance Sheet (in million $)

Assets	2010
Cash	$20
Accounts receivable	$20
Inventories	$60
Total current assets	$100
Plant & equipment (net)	$100
Total assets	$200

Liabilities & Equity

	2010
Accounts payable	$10
Notes payable	$20
Total current liabilities	$30
Long-term bonds	$70
Total liabilities	$100

Stockholders' equity

	2010
Common stock (paid-in capital - 10,000,000 shares)	$20
Retained earnings	$80
Total liabilities & equity	$200

Income Statement (in million $)

	2010
Sales revenue	$300
Operating costs	$272
Earnings before interest, tax, depreciation & ammortization (EBITDA)	$28
Depreciation & amortization expense	$10
Operating income (EBIT)	$18
Interest expense	$7
Profit before tax (PBT)	$11
Income tax expense	$1
Net Income	$10
Common Dividends	$0
Retained earnings	$10

Statement of Cash Flows (in million $)	2010
Net Income	$10
Add: Depreciation & amortization	$10
Subtract: Increase in inventory	($10)
Net cash provided by operating activities	$10
Cash used to acquire long-term assets	($20)
Increase in notes payable	$10
Increase in long-term bonds	$10
Net cash provided by financing activities	$20
Net increase in cash	$10
Opening cash balance	$10
Closing cash balance	$20

Liquidity Ratios

These ratios provide an idea of the liquidity position of a company. They are important to know whether the company would be able to pay off its debts as they become due – interest, loan payments, accounts payable etc. Two liquidity ratios described below are commonly used.

Current Ratio

Current ratio = Current Assets/Current Liabilities

For AllFresh, Current ratio = $100 million/$30 million = 3.33

This means that current assets of AllFresh cover over 3 times its current liability payments.

In order to know whether this value is good or bad one needs to get the industry average figure. We further find that the industry average is 5.0. It means that AllFresh has a lower than average current ratio, which could mean lower than expected liquidity. This ratio is frequently used by lenders, like banks, before extending a loan.

Quick (Acid Test) Ratio

Quick ratio = (Current Assets − Inventories)/Current Liabilities

For AllFresh, Quick ratio = ($100 million − $60 million)/$30 million = 1.33

This ratio assumes that inventory could be difficult to convert into cash at short notice and hence removes it from the current assets for knowing a company's liquidity position.

Once again a comparison is needed with the industry average to compare. If the industry average is 1.0, it means that AllFresh has a stronger liquidity position when computed using quick ratio.

Asset Management Ratios

These ratios show how well the company is managing its assets. These are also called efficiency ratios. Commonly used ones are given below:

Inventory Turnover Ratio

Inventory Turnover ratio = Sales/Inventory

For AllFresh, Inventory Turnover ratio = $300 million/$60 million = 5.0

This ratio tells us how well the company is managing its inventory against the sales it has. We can take an average of the inventory over the year as inventory mentioned in the balance sheet is at a particular point of time and that value could give incorrect results if inventory has suddenly increased or decreased. A higher value of this ratio is generally preferable as it means that the company is holding lower inventory.

If the industry average is 4.0, then AllFresh has a better value of inventory turnover ratio. It means that it is carrying lower inventory than its competitors for the same sales volume.

Days Sales Outstanding

Days Sales Outstanding = Accounts receivable/Sales per day

For AllFresh = $20 million/($300 million/365) = 24.33 days

Days Sales Outstanding (DSO) is the average number of days that a company takes to make collection of its receivables. A lower number means it is able to collect the payments more promptly.

If the industry average is 20 days, then AllFresh is taking longer than other companies and can look at improving the receivables collection mechanism.

Asset Turnover Ratio

Asset Turnover ratio = Sales/Total Assets

For AllFresh = $300 million/$200 million = 1.5

Every company invests in assets in order to generate sales and profits. This measure is about how successful the company is in doing this. A higher asset turnover ratio indicates better asset utilization.

If the industry is having 1.25 as their average asset turnover ratio, it means that AllFresh is better than other companies in producing sales from its assets.

Leverage (Debt Management) Ratios

Companies have mainly two modes of raising capital – debt and equity. Both ways have their pros and cons which will be discussed in the later chapters. Lenders and investors use debt management ratios to see how risky the company's capital structure is and how it stands against the industry's norms. Below are the most frequently used ratios:

Debt Ratio

Debt ratio = Total Liabilities/Total Assets

For AllFresh, Debt ratio = $100 million/$200 million = 0.5 or 50%

This ratio tells the company's creditors and lenders how risky it is to lend to the company. They would prefer a lower debt ratio. If the industry average debt ratio is 0.6, then creditors would be happy to lend to AllFresh as it has a lower debt ratio as compared to its competitors. The amount of debt and equity taken by a company largely depends on the industry it belongs to. Some industries, like power production, have several capital assets that can be used to take cheaper secured loans. Hence, they are generally high on debt and therefore have a higher debt ratio. Services industries, on the other hand, have few physical assets that can be mortgaged. Hence, they generally have lower debt ratio.

Debt-to-Equity Ratio

Debt-to-equity ratio = Total Liabilities/Stockholders' Equity

For AllFresh, Debt-to-equity ratio = $100 million/$100 million = 1.0A debt-to-equity ratio of 1.0 means the company has equal amount of liabilities and equity. This ratio is seen by creditors and lenders and they would prefer it to be low. Equity investors of the company would like this to be high as the additional debt (liability) taken by the company can lead to greater profits and hence, better returns for common stockholders. This is called leverage.

Times Interest Earned (TIE)

TIE = EBIT/Interest expense

For AllFresh, TIE = $18 million/$7 million = 2.57

This ratio gives a comparison of the company's earnings against its interest expense for the debt it has taken. In the above case, AllFresh has enough earnings to serve its interest expense 2.57 times. Lenders would like this to be high as it means that they are better covered on the interest payments.

Profitability Ratios

These show how profitable the company is in doing business. Profitability can be computed using various bases – equity, assets and sales. Accordingly, there are several ratios as below:

Return on Equity (ROE)

ROE = Net Income/Stockholders' Equity

For AllFresh, ROE = $10 million/$100 million = 0.1 or 10%

This is the most important and the most frequently looked at ratio. It gives the amount a common stockholder gets when investing in the company. In the above case, a stockholder received 10% returns on his investment in the year 2010. This measure would have a direct impact on the company's stock price.

If the industry average ROE is 9%, then AllFresh is considered to be giving higher returns and hence, would be preferred by stockholders over its competitors.

Return on Assets (ROA)

ROA = Net Income/Total Assets

For AllFresh, ROA = $10 million/$200 million = 0.05 or 5%

This ratio determines how much profit the company is making using the assets it has. It gives the company's efficiency in using its assets.

If the industry average happens to be 7% then AllFresh is not utilizing its assets as well as its competitors.

Return on Sales (ROS)

ROS = Net Income/Sales

For AllFresh, ROS = $10 million/$300 million = 0.0333 or 3.33%

This ratio is often referred to as the sales margin or profit margin. For every dollar of sales, AllFresh is earning about 3 cents. This needs to be seen in light of industry average. Some industries have a lower profit margin but higher sales volume.

If the industry average is 2.5% then AllFresh has a better return on sales.

Basic Earning Power (BEP)

BEP = EBIT/Total Assets

For AllFresh, BEP = $18 million/$200 million = 0.09 or 9%

This ratio shows the raw earning power of a company without getting influenced by its taxes and leverage (debt). Different companies in the same industry may have different tax situations and debt structure. This ratio is useful when comparing such companies.

Market Value Ratios

When a company's stock price is compared to other values, such ratios are called market value ratios. They give useful insight into what the investors think about the company.

Price/Earnings Ratio (P/E)

P/E ratio = Market Price per share/Earnings per share

For AllFresh, assume that the current stock price is $20

Earnings per share = Net Income/Number of common shares = $10 million/10 million = $1

Hence, P/E ratio = $20/$1 = 20

P/E ratio shows how much the investors are willing to pay per dollar of company's profit. A higher P/E ratio means that the investors see strong growth prospects in the company.

If the industry average P/E ratio is 15 then it means that investors are looking at AllFresh to provide better growth than its competitors.

Market/Book Ratio (M/B)

M/B ratio = Market Price per share/Book value per share

For AllFresh, assume current stock price is $20

Book value per share = Total Common Equity/Number of common shares = $100 million/10 million = $10

Hence, M/B ratio = $20/$10 = 2

This ratio is also a measure of how much the investors expect the company to grow and are willing to invest. A higher value of M/B ratio means that the investors are willing to pay more to buy the company's stock.

If the industry average is 1.8 then it means that the investors are willing to pay more for AllFresh than its competitors as they expect better returns.

Cash Flow Ratios

Until now all ratios described above have been either on balance sheets items, income statement items or on the market price of the stock. There are also some important ratios based on cash flows of a company. These ratios give vital information as statement of cash flows is the only financial statement that gives "real" values. Both, balance sheet and income statement have values that are either based on estimates or on historical costs.

Cash Flow to Net Income Ratio

Cash Flow to Net Income ratio = Cash from Operating Activities/Net Income

For AllFresh, Cash Flow to Net Income ratio = $10 million/$10 million = 1

This ratio shows as to what extent the company has used accrual accounting assumptions and adjustments in computing its Net Income. It will generally be equal to or greater than 1 due to non-cash expenses like depreciation and amortization. A company should have a stable cash flow to net income ratio over years unless there has been a significant change in its accounting assumptions.

It may be noted that cash flow from operations is used to compute this ratio. Hence, a lower value of this ratio will also highlight those companies that are not having adequate cash inflow from normal business activities which could lead to cash problems in future.

Cash Flow Adequacy Ratio

Cash Flow Adequacy ratio = Cash from Operating Activities/Cash used in Investing Activities

For AllFresh, Cash Flow Adequacy ratio = $10 million/$20 million = 0.5

This ratio tells us whether a company is able to generate enough cash to pay for all its investing activities. It would be greater than 1 for a "cash cow" that is able to pay for its capital expansion using cash generated from operations alone. It does not need any further financing in form of debt or equity. AllFresh is not a cash cow.

Cash Times Interest Earned Ratio

Cash Times Interest Earned ratio = Cash earned before Interest and Tax/Interest expense where, Cash earned before Interest and Tax = Cash from Operating Activities + Interest expense + Income tax expense

For AllFresh, Cash earned before Interest and Tax = $10 million + $7 million + $1 million = $18 million

Hence, Cash Times Interest Earned ratio = $18 million/$7 million = 2.57

This ratio is similar to TIE described above but it takes cash instead of net income. Hence, this is a more accurate measure of how well can the company covers its interest expenses. AllFresh generates cash that is enough to pay 2.57 times its interest expense for the year. In this case it turns out that AllFresh's TIE ratio and Cash Times Interest Earned ratio are the same. This is because the company has paid the same amount of cash in interest expense and income tax expense as it has accrued in its Income statement.

But these two values could differ and in such cases, Cash Times Interest Earned ratio would give a better visibility to the company's cash strength to pay for interest and income tax.

DuPont Framework

This framework is used to break and analyze a company's Return on Equity (ROE), which is the ultimate ratio that investors look at. Return on Equity is given as:

ROE = Net Income/Stockholders' Equity

A company borrows money from stockholders and invests that in Assets that help the company generate Sales which finally generate profit. This gives us the below three entities:

Borrowing from Stockholders to invest in Assets

Assets-to-Equity ratio = Total Assets/Stockholders' Equity

Assets help generate Sales

Asset Turnover ratio = Sales/Total Assets

Sales generate Profit

Return on Sales = Net Income/Sales

If we combine all the three entities above, we get ROE as below:

ROE = (Net Income/Sales) x (Sales/Total Assets) x (Total Assets/Stockholders' Equity)

The above expanded ROE equation helps us understand where the company needs to improve if its ROE is low. Does the company have lower profitability, or lower efficiency, or lower leverage? It can also be a combination of some or all of these. With this new insight the company can take steps for improvement.

Let's take an example. Company ABC has an ROE of 12%, whereas, its competitor, XYZ, has an ROE of 15%. Company ABC needs to find out how to improve its ROE. Hence, it finds out the three other ratios – Profitability, Efficiency and Leverage. Below is the data available:

Ratio	ABC	XYZ
Profitability	5%	5%
Efficiency	0.8	0.6
Leverage	3.0	5.0

ROE of ABC = 5% x 0.8 x 3.0 = 12%

ROE of XYZ = 5% x 0.6 x 5.0 = 15%

From the above data it is clear that ABC is actually more efficient than XYZ in generating sales for the assets that it holds. Its profitability is also equal to that of XYZ. However, its leverage is lower. This means that ABC is unable to generate enough assets against its equity investment. One way of doing this is by taking up more debt and converting that money into assets. This technique is called leveraging.

Benchmarking

All the ratios seen in the previous section need to be seen with respect to other companies in the same industry. That is when a company can see if it needs to make any changes in its capital structure, margins etc. This activity is called benchmarking. It involves comparison against the best in the industry and trying to match the performance.

Companies also need to continuously benchmark against their own performance over the years. For example, if a company has an ROE of 10% in one year and 8% in the next, it needs to find the reason for this change. Ratios are expected to remain stable across years unless there has been a significant change in the company's business, capital structure or the market itself.

Limitation of Financial Ratios

Although financial ratios are a powerful tool to analyze companies, they come with several limitations as below:

a) Different companies follow different accounting practices. This makes direct comparison difficult. Sometimes, even when a company changes its own accounting practices it becomes difficult to compare with ratios from the previous years.

b) It is often difficult to classify values of ratios as being good or bad. If a company has a lower profit margin (lower ROS) than its competitors it may not always be bad if that lower margin is able to generate higher sales volume.

c) Conglomerates do business in various diversified industries. This makes it difficult to benchmark them against any single industry. Similar difficulty is faced by other companies when trying to benchmark against a conglomerate.

d) Values of assets and liabilities in a company's balance sheet are carried at historical costs. This can bring in significant difference between the ratios of old and new companies.

e) If ratios are computed on a quarterly basis, they could be affected by seasonality or business cycle.

f) Companies often use "window dressing" techniques that could distort financial ratios. For example, borrowing cash for long-term just before the end of the year could increase the company's current ratio. Once the financial statements have been prepared the company may return the loan.

Common-size Financial Statements

Ratio analysis is but one tool for financial statement analysis. However, it may not be enough to analyze a company's finances. Common-size financial statement analysis fills that gap.

This tool helps in comparing a company's financial statements over years and with other companies of different sizes. Consider the below financial statements of AllFresh seen earlier. It now has data for the past two years for comparison.

Balance Sheet (in million $)	2010	2009
Assets		
Cash	$20	$10
Accounts receivable	$20	$20
Inventories	$60	$50
Total current assets	$100	$80
Plant & equipment (net)	$100	$90
Total assets	$200	$170
Liabilities & Equity		
Accounts payable	$10	$10
Notes payable	$20	$10
Total current liabilities	$30	$20
Long-term bonds	$70	$60
Total liabilities	$100	$80
Stockholders' equity		
Common stock (paid-in capital - 10,000,000 shares)	$20	$20
Retained earnings	$80	$70
Total liabilities & equity	$200	$170

Income Statement (in million $)	2010	2009
Sales revenue	$300	$250
Operating costs	$272	$227
EBITDA	$28	$23
Depreciation & amortization expense	$10	$8
Operating income (EBIT)	$18	$15
Interest expense	$7	$5
Profit before tax (PBT)	$11	$10
Income tax expense	$1	$1
Net Income	$10	$9
Common Dividends	$0	$2
Retained earnings	$10	$7

The first step in analyzing using common-size financial statements is to convert the above balance sheet and income statements into common-size formats. In a common-size balance sheet, all values are represented as a percentage of the Total Assets. This tells us in what percentage each asset, liability and equity is divided in the company. In a common-size income statement, all expenses are represented as a percentage of the total revenues. This gives us a view of where the company is spending its money. The balance sheet in common-size format is given below:

Balance Sheet (in million $)	2010	%	2009	%
Assets				
Cash	$20	10.00%	$10	5.88%
Accounts receivable	$20	10.00%	$20	11.76%
Inventories	$60	30.00%	$50	29.41%
Total current assets	$100	50.00%	$80	47.06%
Plant & equipment (net)	$100	50.00%	$90	52.94%
Total assets	$200	100.00%	$170	100.00%
Liabilities & Equity				
Accounts payable	$10	5.00%	$10	5.88%
Notes payable	$20	10.00%	$10	5.88%
Total current liabilities	$30	15.00%	$20	11.76%
Long-term bonds	$70	35.00%	$60	35.29%
Total liabilities	$100	50.00%	$80	47.06%
Stockholders' equity				
Common stock (paid-in capital – 10,000,000 shares)	$20	10.00%	$20	11.76%
Retained earnings	$80	40.00%	$70	41.18%
Total liabilities & equity	$200	100.00%	$170	100.00%

It can be seen that the company has increased its current assets from 47% to 50% from 2009 to 2010. Most of this increase can be attributed to increase in cash. In fact, the company has managed to bring down the percentage of accounts receivable probably by following up on pending dues more rigorously. In the same period it has increased its current liabilities from 12% to 15%. This is mainly due to increased short-term loans in the form of notes. The company's financing mix has also changed from 47:53 (Total Liabilities: Total Equity) to 50:50.

Similarly, the company's income statement in common-size format is shown below:

Income Statement (in million $)	2010	%	2009	%
Sales revenue	$300	100.00%	$250	100.00%
Operating costs	$272	90.67%	$227	90.80%
EBITDA	$28	9.33%	$23	9.20%
Depreciation & amortization expense	$10	3.33%	$8	3.20%
Operating income (EBIT)	$18	6.00%	$15	6.00%
Interest expense	$7	2.33%	$5	2.00%
Profit before tax (PBT)	$11	3.67%	$10	4.00%
Income tax expense	$1	0.33%	$1	0.40%
Net Income	$10	3.33%	$9	3.60%
Common Dividends	$0	0.00%	$2	0.80%
Retained earnings	$10	3.33%	$7	2.80%

Even though the company's revenues have increased, the profits have gone down from 3.6% to 3.33% from 2009 to 2010. This is mainly due to additional interest expense that has gone up from 2% to 2.33% of revenues. The company can use this information to decide whether to go for greater debt funding. If the interest expense would rise further in terms of percentage of revenues then it may reduce the profits. Another thing to note is that the company has managed to reduce its operating costs from 90.8% to 90.67%.

The above analysis can also be done between two or more companies to see how their expenses are in relation to sales and where is an opportunity for improvement.

Solved Examples

2.1 ABC Inc. has the following Balance Sheet at 31st Dec, 2010:

Assets

Current assets	
Cash	$50,000
Accounts receivable	(a)
Total current assets	(b)
Long-term investments	$40,000
Property, plant, and equipment	$100,000
Total assets	(c)

Liabilities and Stockholders' Equity

Current liabilities	
Accounts payable	(d)
Short-term loans	$30,000
Total current liabilities	$40,000
Long-term liabilities	(e)
Total liabilities	(f)
Stockholders' equity	
Paid-in capital	$35,000
Retained earnings	(g)
Total stockholders' equity	(h)
Total liabilities and stockholders' equity	(i)

Following information is also available:

Current ratio = 1.5

Debt ratio = 60%

Compute all the missing values in the Balance Sheet.

Solution:

d = $40,000 - $30,000 = $10,000

Current ratio = Current assets/Current liabilities

Therefore, 1.5 = b/$40,000. This gives, b = $60,000.

Further, b = $50,000 + a. This gives, a = $10,000.

Total assets, c = b + $40,000 + $100,000 = $200,000

Total liabilities and equity = i = Total assets = $200,000

Debt ratio = Total liabilities/Total assets

Hence, Debt ratio = Total liabilities/Total assets

0.6 = f/$200,000. This gives, f = $120,000.

Further, e = $40,000 + f = $160,000

Also, h = i − f = $200,000 - $160,000 = $40,000

And g = h - $35,000 = $5,000

2.2 Following data has been given for XYZ Inc.:

Market value of stocks	$500,000
Total liabilities	$200,000
Debt ratio	25%
ROS	12%
Asset turnover ratio	3

Find out Total assets, Sales, Net Income and P/E ratio.

Solution:

Debt ratio = Total liabilities/Total assets

Hence, Total assets = $200,000/0.25 = $800,000

Asset turnover ratio = Sales/Total assets

Hence, Sales = 3 x $800,000 = $2,400,000

ROS = Net Income/Sales

Hence, Net Income = 12% x $2,400,000 = $288,000

P/E ratio = Price per share/Earnings per share

We don't know the number of shares so it is not possible to compute values per share. However, we know the total market value and total earnings.

Hence, P/E ratio = $500,000/$288,000 = 1.74

2.3 Two companies, ABC Inc. and XYZ Inc., have the following information:

	ABC Inc.	XYZ Inc.
Current assets	$15,000	$60,000
Long-term assets	$20,000	$120,000
Current liabilities	$8,000	$50,000
Long-term liabilities	$15,000	$100,000
Sales	$200,000	$800,000
Net Income	$5,000	$10,000
Market price per share	$20	$50
Number of shares	5,000	2,000

a) Find the following:

   Current ratio

   Debt ratio

   ROS

   Asset turnover ratio

   ROE

   P/E ratio

b) Comment on the health of the two companies and compare their profitability.

Solution:

a) Below are the ratio computations:

Ratio		ABC Inc.	XYZ Inc.
Current ratio	Current assets/Current liabilities	1.88	1.20
Debt ratio	Total liabilities/Total assets	0.66	0.83
ROS	Net Income/Sales	2.50%	1.25%
Asset turnover ratio	Sales/Total assets	5.71	4.44
ROE	Net Income/Total equity Total equity = Total assets - Total liabilities	8.62%	3.03%
P/E ratio	Price per share/Earnings per share	20.00	10.00

b) XYZ Inc. has greater sales and greater assets. However, when looking at the ratios, it is clear that ABC Inc., although a leaner company, is better in almost all respects. It has better current ratio (liquidity), lower debt, is more efficient (higher asset turnover) and greater profitability (higher ROE). The market also has higher expectations from ABC Inc., as seen from a higher P/E ratio.

2.4 Below is the Income Statement of ZZZ Inc.:

	2010	2009
Sales	$300,000	$275,000
Cost of goods sold	$220,000	$150,000
Gross profit	$80,000	$125,000
Selling, general, and administrative expense	$50,000	$70,000
Operating Income (EBIT)	$30,000	$55,000
Interest expense	$35,000	$25,000
Profit (loss) before Tax (PBT)	($5,000)	$30,000
Income tax expense (refund)	($2,000)	$10,000
Net Income	($3,000)	$20,000

a) Prepare common-size income statement.

b) Why did ZZZ Inc.'s profitability reduce significantly during 2010?

c) ZZZ Inc.'s operating income is lower than its interest expense. Does this mean that the company was unable to pay interest to its debtors?

Solution:

a) Below is the common-size income statement:

	2010	%	2009	%
Sales	$300,000	100%	$275,000	100%
Cost of goods sold	$220,000	73%	$150,000	55%
Gross profit	$80,000	27%	$125,000	45%
Selling, general, and administrative expense	$50,000	17%	$70,000	25%
Operating Income (EBIT)	$30,000	10%	$55,000	20%
Interest expense	$35,000	12%	$25,000	9%
Profit (loss) before Tax (PBT)	($5,000)	-2%	$30,000	11%
Income tax expense (refund)	($2,000)	-1%	$10,000	4%
Net Income	($3,000)	-1%	$20,000	7%

b) ZZZ Inc. had significantly higher cost of goods sold in 2010 as compared to 2009. This brought down the profitability in 2010.

c) Operating income is only an estimate of the profits made from operations of the company. Interest expense can be higher than that as it is paid through the company's cash balance. If the company has enough cash balance then it can still pay interest to its debtors.

Practice Exercise

2.1 The following information is available about two companies, ABC Inc. and XYZ Inc.:

Both the companies have the same total assets

ABC Inc. has a higher total asset turnover ratio than XYZ Inc.

ABC Inc. has a higher profit margin than XYZ Inc.

XYZ Inc. has higher inventory turnover ratio than ABC Inc.

XYZ Inc. has higher current ratio than ABC Inc.

Which of the following statements is correct?

a) ABC Inc. must have a higher Net Income

b) ABC Inc. must have a higher ROE

c) XYZ Inc. must have a higher ROA

d) Statements a and b are correct

e) Statements a and c are correct

2.2 Following information is available for AAA Inc. and ZZZ Inc.:

	AAA Inc.	ZZZ Inc.
Assets	$1,629,304	$13,084
Equity	$932,389	$4,301
Sales	$2,414,415	$12,261
Net Income	$109,617	$1,551

a) Calculate ROS for both companies.

b) Which of the following statements is true?

  i. AAA Inc. has weaker ROE but a stronger asset-to-equity ratio

  ii. AAA Inc. has a weaker ROE but a stronger ROS

iii. AAA Inc. has a weaker ROE but a stronger asset turnover ratio

iv. AAA Inc. has a stronger ROE but a weaker asset turnover ratio

2.3 ABC Inc. has a DSO of 30 days. Company has sales of $5 million per year. What is the company's accounts receivable?

2.4 Following information is available for XYZ Inc.:

Asset turnover ratio = 1.5

ROA = 4%

ROE = 6%

Calculate the company's profit margin and debt ratio.

2.5 Below is the Income Statement of ZZZ Inc. for the past two years:

	2010	2009
Sales	$2,000,000	$1,130,000
Cost of goods sold	$1,020,000	$480,000
Gross profit	$980,000	$650,000
Selling, general, and administrative expenses	$250,000	$200,000
Operating income (EBIT)	$730,000	$450,000
Interest expense	$100,000	$80,000
Profit before tax (PBT)	$630,000	$370,000
Income tax expense	$220,000	$130,000
Net Income	$410,000	$240,000

a) Prepare common-size income statements.

b) Has the Net Income increased from 2009 to 2010 in relative terms (relative to sales)?

Chapter 3

Cost of Capital

Companies need to raise capital to conduct business. They use capital to invest in assets that help them generate sales. There are three basic ways using which companies borrow capital – debt, preferred stock, and common stock. Retained earnings is another source of capital, generally the largest for profitable companies. In the sections below we describe the cost of raising money through each of these means and how a company calculates its total cost of capital. This information is used to make capital budgeting decisions for deciding which projects to undertake.

Cost of Debt (k_d)

Debt funding is a loan taken from another party that has a certain rate of interest to be paid at fixed intervals. For example, consider a company taking a $1 million loan from a bank at 10% with interest to be paid yearly. It would have to pay $100,000 interest every year. This amount is the cost of debt – 10%. This is the before-tax cost of debt. However, companies are allowed to deduct the interest paid in their income statement. Hence, the after-tax cost of debt will be lower due to reduced tax burden because of the interest payment. If in the above example, the company has an effective tax rate of 40%, then the cost of debt would be as below:

Cost of debt = 10% - Tax saving due to interest expense = 10% - (40% of 10%) = 6%

The before-tax cost of debt is referred to as k_d and the tax rate as T to give the cost of debt as:

Cost of debt = $k_d(1 - T)$

It needs to be noted that the above cost of debt is assuming that the company is having profit. If it is running losses, then its effective tax rate would be zero, thereby making $T = 0$. This means that the before-tax and after-tax cost of debt is the same for such a company.

Cost of Preferred Stock (k_p)

Preferred stock is in many ways similar to debt funding.

However, a company's inability to pay preferred dividends to its preferred stockholders does not automatically lead it to bankruptcy, nor does the company get to deduct these dividends while computing their net income.

Let's say that a company has issued preferred stock to its shareholders for $100 per share (referred to as P_p) that pays a fixed dividend (dividends on preferred stock are fixed like interest rate on debt) of $10 (referred to as D_p), then the cost of preferred stock is:

Cost of preferred stock = $k_p = D_p/P_p$ = \$10/\$100 = 0.1 or 10%

Cost of Retained Earnings (k_s)

Retained earnings are the profits of the company that are ploughed back into the business (or retained by the company). They are the biggest source of capital for profitable companies and belong to the common stockholders of the company. Although this form of funding does not require any actual borrowing, it still comes at a cost. This is called Opportunity cost. If the company had not retained the amount then they would have distributed it amongst the common stockholders. The stockholders could then invest it elsewhere and earn interest or capital gain. But by retaining the earnings, the company has prevented the stockholders from this earning and hence, there is an Opportunity cost associated with this retained amount. Cost of Retained Earnings (k_s) can be calculated using three different ways as described in the sections below.

Bond-Yield-Plus-Risk-Premium Approach

If a company issues bonds to raise capital, then this approach can be used to estimate its cost of retained earnings. Bonds are fixed interest bearing instruments, whereas, common equity (or simply, equity) is traded on the stock exchange and its return depends upon the company's performance. Since bonds give a fixed assured interest, they are less risky than equity. So in order to calculate the company's cost of equity (retained earnings), a certain risk premium needs to be added as the shareholders are taking a risk that is higher than when they invest in the company's bonds. This is because bonds give a fixed assured interest, whereas, equity does not give any assurance of fixed income. Hence, cost of retained earnings using this approach is as given below:

k_s = Bond yield + Risk premium

Let's say that a company issues bonds at 9% and the risk premium is estimated to be 5%, then the cost of retained earnings is:

k_s = 9% + 5% = 14%

The risk premium of 5% is an estimated value that comes from judgement by analysts and investors that are aware of the company's business risks.

Capital Asset Pricing Model (CAPM) Approach

This approach of estimating cost of retained earnings is similar to the bond-yield-plus-risk-premium approach but uses a less judgemental way of calculating the risk premium. Instead of taking the returns of a company's own bonds, it takes the returns given by relatively risk-free bonds, like US Treasury bonds, as its bottom line. Then it applies two types of premiums to it – market risk premium and company's business risk premium. Below equation is used in the CAPM approach for estimating the cost of retained earnings:

$k_s = k_{RF} + (k_M - k_{RF}) \times b_i$

k_{RF} – Risk-free return of bonds like those issued by US Treasury

k_M – Market return of the average stock. This is a purely market dependent variable. During a bull run, this can go high and during a bear run, it would be lower.

b_i – Beta coefficient of the company. This is an index that shows the company's riskiness. When a company's stock is expected to have about the same risk as an average stock in the market, $b_i = 1$. If it is riskier, $b_i > 1$. If it is less risky, $b_i < 1$.

Let's say that 30-day US treasury bills have an interest rate of 6%. Also assume that we have estimated that an average stock on the stock market will return 10% and that the company's stock is less risky than an average stock and stands at about $b_i = 0.8$. Then the cost of retained earnings is as given below:

$k_s = 6\% + (10\% - 6\%) \times 0.8 = 9.2\%$

The biggest challenge in computing cost of retained earnings using CAPM is the calculation of k_M and b_i. Further, there is also confusion on whether to use risk-free returns of long-term bonds or short-term bonds.

Discounted Cash Flow (DCF) Approach

Common stockholders, who own Retained Earnings portion of the company, look for two types of returns. First is in the form of dividends and the other is in the form of capital gains. This expectation is used in this approach to calculate cost of retained earnings as below:

k_s = Dividend yield + Capital gains

Dividend yield = D_1/P_0

Where, D_1 = expected dividends at the end of year 1

And, P_0 = price of the company's common stock today

Capital gains = Growth rate of the company = g

This gives, $k_s = (D_1/P_0) + g$

It needs to be noted that both dividend and growth rates are expected rates. Let's take example of a company whose share is currently selling at $20 and looking at past years, it is expected to give $1 dividend at the end of this year and its stock price is expected to grow by 5% this year. Then its cost of retained earnings will be:

$k_s = (\$1/\$20) + 5\% = 10\%$

Cost of New Common Stock (k_e)

When a company issues new common stock, it incurs a flotation cost. This includes fees paid to investment bankers who help in issuing the new stock on the stock exchange. Due to this, cost of new common stock is more than cost of retained earnings discussed earlier. Apart from that, both new common stock and retained earnings have the same cost of capital. If we use the Discounted Cash Flow (DCF) method to estimate the cost of new common stock, it is given as:

$k_e = (D_1/(P_0 x (1 - F))) + g$

Where, F is the flotation cost

Let's take the same example as above where the company's next dividend is expected to $1 and the stock price is expected to grow by 5%. Let's also say that company does not have enough Retained Earnings to satisfy its capital requirements and hence decides to issue new common stock at $20. Due this new stock offer, it would incur a flotation cost, say 10% of its offering of $20. Then the cost of new common stock is given as:

$k_e = (\$1/(\$20 \times (1 - 10\%))) + 5\% = 0.056 + 5\% = 5.6\% + 5\% = 10.6\%$

As seen above, the cost of new common equity is a little higher than cost of retained earnings due to the additional flotation costs.

Weighted Average Cost of Capital (WACC)

Most companies raise capital through multiple means – debt, preferred stock and common stock. Hence, if the company wants to calculate its total cost of capital, it would need to calculate the cost of capital of each of these and then arrive at a composite figure, called Weighted Average Cost of Capital or WACC.

Depending upon the capital structure of a company, it would assign weights to each form of funding, like 50% debt, 10% preferred stock and 40% common stock. Then using these weights the company can calculate its WACC. Below is an example.

Cost of capital for each form of capital is as below. We assume that the company does not issue any new common equity. The 40% common stock is in the form of retained earnings.

$k_d = 8\%$

$k_p = 9\%$

$k_s = 10\%$

Also consider effective tax rate to be 40%. Now, in order to calculate the WACC we do the following:

$WACC = w_d k_d (1 - T) + w_p k_p + w_s k_s$

$= 50\% \times 8\% (1 - 40\%) + 10\% \times 9\% + 40\% \times 10\% = 2.4\% + 0.9\% + 4\%$

$= 7.3\%$

This is the cost of capital that the company would use in capital budgeting to decide whether projects should be taken up or not. This figure is also called a "hurdle rate" that projects need to cross in order to be taken up by the company. In the above example, all projects giving a return of more than 7.3% would be taken up and those returning lesser would be rejected.

The above mentioned hurdle rate applies to projects that are of average risk for the company. But if the company is evaluating taking up a project that is riskier than its average project, then it would use a hurdle rate that is higher than its WACC. Similarly, for a lower risk project it would use a hurdle rate that is lower than its WACC. This is because WACC only applies to projects of average risk for a company and needs adjustment for risk.

Similar adjustment of WACC is needed in multi-division companies where some divisions inherently have lower risk projects or higher risk projects when compared to an average project of the company. Instead of using the company's WACC, divisions would devise a WACC for themselves.

Solved Examples

3.1 ABC Inc. can issue preferred stock at a price of $50 per share. These are expected to pay a yearly dividend of $4 per share. What is the company's cost of preferred stock?

Solution:

Cost of preferred stock, k_p

$= D_1/P_0$

$= \$4/\$50$

$= 8\%$

3.2 XYZ Inc. is expected to issue a dividend of $3 per share to its common stockholders at the end of the year. Analysts expect the company to have a growth rate of 7% of the current stock price of $40. If new stock is issued by the company, then it will get only $35 per share due to flotation costs.

a) **Calculate cost of retained earnings of the company.**

b) **Calculate the percentage of flotation cost of the company.**

c) **Calculate the cost of new common stock issued by the company.**

Solution:

a) Cost of retained earnings, k_s

    $= (D_1/P_0) + g$

    $= (\$3/\$40) + 7\%$

    $= 14.5\%$

b) Flotation cost $= \$40 - \$35 = \$5$

    Percentage of flotation cost $= \$5/\$40 = 12.5\%$

c) Cost of new common stock, k_e

    $= (D_1/P_0 \times (1 - F)) + g$

    $= (\$3/\$40 \times (1 - 12.5\%)) + 7\%$

    $= 8.57\% + 7\%$

    $= 15.57\%$

3.3 Below is the Balance Sheet of ZZZ Inc. The company has cost of common stock as 15% and before-tax cost of debt as 10%. The company's tax rate is 30%. Calculate the company's WACC.

Assets	
Cash	$50,000
Accounts receivable	$100,000
Inventories	$350,000
Plant, property, and equipment	$1,000,000
Total assets	**$1,500,000**
Liabilities and Stockholders' equity	
Accounts payable	$200,000
Long-term debt	$520,000
Common equity	$780,000
Total liabilities and equity	**$1,500,000**

Solution:

Cost of debt before tax, $k_d = 10\%$

Cost of debt after tax, $k_d \times (1 - T) = 10\% \times (1 - 30\%) = 7\%$

Cost of common equity = $k_e = 15\%$

Total capital of the company = $520,000 + $780,000 = $1,300,000

Weight of debt capital = $520,000/$1,300,000 = 40\%

Weight of common equity capital = $780,000/$1,300,000 = 60\%

Therefore, WACC

$= w_d k_d \times (1 - T) + w_e k_e$

$= 40\% \times 7\% + 60\% \times 15\%$

$= 2.8\% + 9\% = 11.8\%$

3.4 Company AAA Inc. has a WACC of 12.75%. The company is considering taking up the following projects. All of them are equivalent to the riskiness of the company's existing assets. Which ones should the company take up?

Project	Investment	Rate of Return
A	$10,000	12%
B	$100,000	12.5%
C	$1 million	13%
D	$1 million	15%
E	$10 million	13.5%

Solution:

Since the company's WACC is 12.75%, it should only accept projects that cross this hurdle rate, irrespective of the investment size as long as they are as risky as the company's average project. Since all the above projects are having average risk, the only decision variable is the rate of return; investment size is irrelevant..

Only projects C, D & E have a higher return than the WACC. Hence, only they should be taken up.

Practice Exercise

3.1 ABC Inc. has a capital structure consisting 40% debt and 60% common equity. It's before-tax cost of debt is 10% and the tax rate is 30%. The company's stock is currently selling at $25. The company had issued a dividend of $2.5 per share last year which is expected to grow by 5% this year and so is the company's stock price. What is the company's WACC?

3.2 Following information is available about XYZ Inc.:

a) The company's capital structure is 70% equity and 30% debt

b) The yield on company's bonds is 9%

c) The company is expected to give a dividend of $0.80 at the end of the year

d) Growth rate is expected to be 9%

e) Current stock price is $25

f) Tax rate applicable is 40%

g) Flotation cost on new common stock will be 10%

Calculate the company's WACC.

3.3 AAA Inc. has a WACC of 12%. The company is looking to take up the projects given below. It has a policy to do risk adjustment by either reducing 2.5% from WACC or adding the same amount to handle projects of lower or higher than average risk respectively. Which projects should be taken up by the company?

Project	Investment	Rate of Return	Risk
A	$1 million	13%	Average
B	$1 million	11.5%	Low
C	$10 million	13.5%	High
D	$100,000	15%	High
E	$250,000	9%	Low

Chapter **4**

Capital Budgeting

Investment decisions involving fixed assets are called Capital Budgeting. These assets are of long-term nature and are expected to help the company to generate cash flows in future. Decisions related to these assets are of utmost importance to companies in several ways. Firstly, due to the long-term nature of these assets they will have an impact on the company's cash flows for a long time in future, generally ranging from a few years to several decades. Secondly, if the company does not take correct capital budgeting decisions, then the competition could take away market share and the company could lose out or even be led to bankruptcy. Finally, due to the long-term nature of capital assets, the company needs to do long-term forecast of demand. Too much deviation in the forecast could lead to unnecessary investment and the ensuing depreciation expense could bring the company's net income down for several years.

Free Cash Flow

When making capital budgeting decisions companies use free cash flow to check whether the investment is worth making. Free cash flow is the cash that remains for distribution to all investors, stockholders and debtors, after the company has made all investments in fixed assets, and in additional working capital needed to run its operations. For making capital budgeting decisions companies use only the free cash flow that is relevant to that capital investment.

In order to calculate the free cash flow (FCF) we first need to compute the after-tax operating profit as below:

Net operating profit after-tax (NOPAT) = EBIT x (1 – T)

Where, EBIT is the Earnings before interest and tax

and T is the rate of income tax

When calculating EBIT, depreciation expense has already been subtracted from the revenue. This means EBIT has been reduced by the depreciation amount even though the company does not actually pay any cash for it. Hence, in order to get an idea of the company's cash flows, this expense will have to be adjusted by adding it back to NOPAT as it is a non-cash expense. There is no outflow of cash that is related to depreciation expense. This gives us the Operating cash flow as below:

Operating cash flow = NOPAT + Depreciation = EBIT x (1 – T) + Depreciation

After we remove the investment in capital assets and in operating working capital, we get the FCF as below:

FCF = Operating cash flow – Capital expenditure – Change in net operating working capital

Therefore, the full formula for FCF is:

FCF = EBIT x (1 – T) + Depreciation – Capital expenditure – Change in net operating working capital

The above FCF formula is applied to cash flows over the years that the project is expected to have cash inflows and outflows. For example, as the capital budgeting project starts, it needs a huge cash outflow for buying fixed assets and in working capital. Hence, FCF in the beginning would be:

FCF (for Year 0) = – Capital expenditure – Change in net operating working capital

Note that there will be no revenue or operating expense right at the project start. It will start having these after the first day of the project. Hence, there is no "EBIT x (1 – T)" in the above formula. These are called cash flows for "Year 0".

Over the years when the project is active, it will have cash inflows in the form of revenues and outflows in the form of operating expenses. Hence, during these years the FCF would be:

FCF (for Year 1 onwards) = EBIT x (1 – T)

Note that the above equation assumes that there will be no further investment in fixed assets or change in operating working capital over the years. Hence, there is no "Capital expenditure" or "Change in net operating working capital" in the above formula.

Finally, in the terminal year, generally the net operating working capital is returned and salvage, if any, of fixed assets is also received. All of these form the FCF for the final year after tax adjustments.

In case the salvage value is higher than the remaining book value then tax will have to be paid on the capital gains. On the contrary, if the salvage value is less than the remaining book value then tax credit can be taken if the company has tax liability in other parts of its business. These tax effects have to be considered in calculating the terminal year cash flows.

Timing of Cash Flows

Once we determine the free cash flow as per the previous section, we also need to determine their timing. Cash that comes in at the end of Year 1 has different significance than the cash that comes at the end of Year 5. For example, if a company is expecting to receive $1 million at the end of this year, that would be more valuable than receiving the same amount after 5 years. This is due to time value of money. The $1 million that the company gets this year can be invested and would become much more after 5 years. Hence, the value of $1 million received after 5 years is much less than the value of the same amount received this year.

Estimating Cash Flows over Life of Project

As seen in previous sections, the two important aspects of capital budgeting are estimating cash flows and their timing. Cash flows would include the following items:

a) **Initial investment outlay** – this is the initial upfront investment on the fixed assets and working capital

b) **Operating cash flows over the project's life** – these are the incremental cash inflows and outflows. In order to get net operating cash flow, we add back the depreciation to after-tax operating income. This will be clear in the example below.

c) **Terminal year cash flows** – these are the cash flows that are received at the end of the project due to salvage value and return of working capital

Let's take an example of a company evaluating a new product manufacturing project. Below are its cash flow estimates in the beginning of the project (initial investment outlay):

a) Cost of new plant - $100,000

b) Cost of new equipments - $25,000

c) Increase in net operating working capital - $10,000

The project will generate products that the company expects to sell over a 3 year period, after which the product would need further refinement. The company is expecting the following to happen over the three years:

a) Units sold per year – 10,000

b) Selling price per unit - $20

c) Variable cost per unit - $12

d) Fixed operating costs per year - $20,000

The depreciation of both plant and equipments is expected to be straight-line over a period of 5 years. Both plant and equipments will be sold at the end of 3 years at their remaining book value. The working capital invested in the beginning of the project will also be recovered at the end of 3 years.

Below sheet shows the input data:

Plant cost (straight-line depreciation over 5 years)	$100,000
Equipment cost (straight-line depreciation over 5 years)	$25,000
Net Operating Working Capital	$10,000
Units sold per year	10,000
Selling price per unit	$20
Variable cost per unit	$12
Fixed operating costs per year	$20,000

Below sheet shows the depreciation schedule of the plant and equipments:

	Years			Cumulative Depreciation
	1	2	3	
Plant				
Depreciation percentage	20%	20%	20%	
Depreciation	$20,000	$20,000	$20,000	$60,000
Ending Book Value	$80,000	$60,000	$40,000	
Equipment				
Depreciation percentage	20%	20%	20%	
Depreciation	$5,000	$5,000	$5,000	$15,000
Ending Book Value	$20,000	$15,000	$10,000	

The cash flows over the years are as shown below:

	Years			
	0	**1**	**2**	**3**
Initial Investment outlay				
Plant	($100,000)			
Equipment	($25,000)			
Increase in net operating working capital	($10,000)			
Total investment	($135,000)			
Operating cash flows over life of project				
Units sold		10,000	10,000	10,000
Selling price per unit		$20	$20	$20
Sales revenue		$200,000	$200,000	$200,000
Variable costs		($120,000)	($120,000)	($120,000)
Fixed operating costs		($20,000)	($20,000)	($20,000)
Depreciation (plant & equipment)		($25,000)	($25,000)	($25,000)
Operating income (EBIT)		$35,000	$35,000	$35,000
Taxes (@ 40%)		($14,000)	($14,000)	($14,000)
Net Operating Profit After Tax (NOPAT)		$21,000	$21,000	$21,000
Add back Depreciation		$25,000	$25,000	$25,000
Operating cash flow		$46,000	$46,000	$46,000
Terminal Year cash flows				
Salvage value				$50,000
Return of net operating working capital				$10,000
Total terminal cash flows				$60,000
Net cash flow	($135,000)	$46,000	$46,000	$106,000

Once the cash flows are estimated as above, there are several ways to make capital budgeting decisions. These methods use the cash flows to make a decision using different criteria. These methods are payback period, discounted payback period, net present value, internal rate of return and modified internal rate of return. Each of these is described in the sections below.

Payback Period

The time required to recover the investment made is called payback period. In order to find out the payback period one needs to know the cash flows over the years and the initial investment. Let's assume that a company has estimated the cash flows as given below for two of its projects:

	Years				
	0	1	2	3	4
Project A					
Net cash flow	($10,000)	$3,000	$5,000	$4,000	$3,000
Project B					
Net cash flow	($5,000)	$1,000	$1,000	$2,000	$3,000

In order to calculate the payback period we need to find the cumulative net cash flows over the years as below:

	Years				
	0	1	2	3	4
Project A					
Net cash flow	($10,000)	$3,000	$5,000	$4,000	$3,000
Cumulative Net cash flow	($10,000)	($7,000)	($2,000)	$2,000	$5,000
Project B					
Net cash flow	($5,000)	$1,000	$1,000	$2,000	$3,000
Cumulative Net cash flow	($5,000)	($4,000)	($3,000)	($1,000)	$2,000

As seen above, the company is able to recover its investment on Project A in year 3 and on Project B in year 4. The complete recovery is in the year when the cumulative net cash flow turns positive. In order to calculate the exact payback period we assume that the cash flows are evenly distributed across the year and use the following formula:

Payback = Year before full recovery + (Unrecovered cost/Cash flow in the year)

Payback of Project A = 2 + ($2,000/$4,000) = 2.5 years

Payback of Project B = 3 + ($1,000/$3,000) = 3.33 years

Considering the cash flows from the example in the previous section, we get the following:

| | **Years** | | | |
	0	**1**	**2**	**3**
Net cash flow	($135,000)	$46,000	$46,000	$106,000
Cumulative Net cash flow	($135,000)	($89,000)	($43,000)	$63,000

Payback period = 2 + ($43,000/$106,000) = 2.41 years

This method gives an idea about the liquidity and riskiness of a project but ignores cash flows after payback. Hence, it is not very effective in deciding which project is more profitable and hence, worth investing. It also does not consider cost of capital of the company while finding the payback period. In reality, a company will have a longer payback period if this cost is considered. The next method, discounted payback period, considers this aspect.

Discounted Payback Period

This is same as the payback period but also gives due consideration to the cost of capital. Each year's net cash flow is discounted by the cost of capital to get discounted net cash flow. These are then added to get a Cumulative discounted net cash flow. The same example is used as above with a cost of capital of 10%.

In order to discount the cash flow, the following formula is used:

Discounted net cash flow = Net cash flow/$(1 + k)^t$

Where, k is the cost of capital and t is the year in which the cash flow is generated.

For example, to calculate the discounted net cash flow in year 1 for Project A, we do the following:

Discounted net cash flow for Project A (Year 1) = $3,000/$(1 + 0.1)^1$ = $2,727.27

Below is the calculation of the Discounted net cash flow for Project A and Project B:

		Years			
	0	1	2	3	4
Project A					
Net cash flow	($10,000)	$3,000	$5,000	$4,000	$3,000
Discounted net cash flow (@10%)	($10,000)	$2,727	$4,132	$3,005	$2,049
Project B					
Net cash flow	($5,000)	$1,000	$1,000	$2,000	$3,000
Discounted net cash flow (@10%)	($5,000)	$909	$826	$1,503	$2,049

Then the Cumulative discounted net cash flow is found as below:

		Years			
	0	1	2	3	4
Project A					
Net cash flow	($10,000)	$3,000	$5,000	$4,000	$3,000
Discounted net cash flow (@10%)	($10,000)	$2,727	$4,132	$3,005	$2,049
Cumulative Discounted net cash flow	($10,000)	($7,273)	($3,140)	($135)	$1,914
Project B					
Net cash flow	($5,000)	$1,000	$1,000	$2,000	$3,000
Discounted net cash flow (@10%)	($5,000)	$909	$826	$1,503	$2,049
Cumulative Discounted net cash flow	($5,000)	($4,091)	($3,264)	($1,762)	$287

We use the same formula to find out the payback period, but this time use Cumulative Discounted net cash flow as below:

Discounted Payback of Project A = 3 + ($135/$2,049) = 3.07 years

Discounted Payback of Project B = 3 + ($1,762/$2,049) = 3.86 years

Since we have discounted the cash flows, the payback period has also got extended.

Applying this method to the cash flows from the previous section gives the following:

	Years			
	0	**1**	**2**	**3**
Net cash flow	($135,000)	$46,000	$46,000	$106,000
Discounted net cash flow (@10%)	($135,000)	$41,818	$38,017	$79,639
Cumulative Discounted net cash flow	($135,000)	($93,182)	($55,165)	$24,474

Discounted Payback period = 2 + ($55,165/$79,639) = 2.69 years

Net Present Value (NPV)

This is the most popular and useful method in taking capital budgeting decisions. It calculates the current (or present) value of future cash flows. It is like saying how much the cash flows over the life of the project are worth today. NPV also starts with the net cash flows as in the above sections. These are then discounted using the project's cost of capital like in the Discounted payback period method. Then all these are added together to find the NPV of the project. Below is the NPV of Projects A and B seen above:

	Years				
	0	1	2	3	4
Project A					
Net cash flow	($10,000)	$3,000	$5,000	$4,000	$3,000
Discounted net cash flow (@10%)	($10,000)	$2,727	$4,132	$3,005	$2,049
NPV	$1,914				
Project B					
Net cash flow	($5,000)	$1,000	$1,000	$2,000	$3,000
Discounted net cash flow (@10%)	($5,000)	$909	$826	$1,503	$2,049
NPV	$287				

There is also an easier way of calculating NPV using Microsoft Excel. Excel has a function called NPV that can be used as below to give the same results as above:

	Years				
	0	1	2	3	4
Project A					
Net cash flow	($10,000)	$3,000	$5,000	$4,000	$3,000
NPV(=NPV(10%, C4:F4) + B4)	$1,914				
Project B					
Net cash flow	($5,000)	$1,000	$1,000	$2,000	$3,000
NPV(=NPV(10%, C7:F7) + B7)	$287				

Similarly, the NPV of the example in the previous section is as below:

	Years			
	0	1	2	3
Net cash flow	($135,000)	$46,000	$46,000	$106,000
NPV (@10% cost of capital)	$24,474			

However, if we find the NPV for the same example at a cost of capital of 20%, then we get the following:

	Years			
	0	**1**	**2**	**3**
Net cash flow	($135,000)	$46,000	$46,000	$106,000
NPV (@20% cost of capital)	($3,380)			

The NPV at 20% cost of capital is -$3,380, showing that the project is not worth taking as it would lead to reduction in stockholders' wealth.

NPV is also used to select from within mutually exclusive projects. If there are 5 potential projects and the company can only invest in 2, it will select the ones with the highest NPV. For independent projects, all those projects that have a positive NPV can be selected by the company as they will be able to recover the cost of capital and also generate additional cash.

Internal Rate of Return (IRR)

Although NPV is the most popular method in selecting capital projects, it does not provide an idea about the returns of a project. It only says whether a project has positive NPV or negative NPV. Hence, several companies also use IRR for capital budgeting decisions as it gives an idea about the expected returns of a project.

IRR also needs net cash flows to start with. It is best to calculate IRR using Microsoft Excel as shown below. We use the excel formula, "IRR", as shown in the cell A5 below:

	Years				
	0	**1**	**2**	**3**	**4**
Project A					
Net cash flow	($10,000)	$3,000	$5,000	$4,000	$3,000
IRR (=IRR(B4:F4))	18.59%				
Project B					
Net cash flow	($5,000)	$1,000	$1,000	$2,000	$3,000
IRR (=IRR(B7:F7))	12.16%				

Project A gives a return of 18.59%, whereas, Project B gives a 12.16% return. Hence, if they are mutually exclusive, then Project A should be selected. Below is the IRR for the other example project:

	Years			
	0	**1**	**2**	**3**
Net cash flow	($135,000)	$46,000	$46,000	$106,000
IRR	18.61%			

The IRR of 18.61% above should be higher than the cost of capital for the project to be accepted. If the cost of capital is 10% then there is good safety margin. However, if the cost of capital is 18% then the project is risky to undertake as a small deviation in the estimated cash flows could make the project give a return lower than the cost of capital.

There are some issues with project selection when using IRR for mutually exclusive projects. Projects of different sizes or those with different cash flow timings can lead to an incorrect project selection decision when using IRR. In such cases NPV is a better option to make a decision. There are also cases when a project has multiple IRRs. This happens when there are large cash outflows in the later years of the project. Once again, in such cases NPV is a better measure to use.

Modified Internal Rate of Return (MIRR)

In order to resolve the above issues with IRR, another method called Modified IRR has been developed. MIRR for a project is calculated using the MIRR function in Microsoft Excel as shown below. We use the excel formula, "MIRR", as shown in cell A5 below:

	Years				
	0	1	2	3	4
Project A					
Net cash flow	($10,000)	$3,000	$5,000	$4,000	$3,000
MIRR (=MIRR(B4:F4, 10%, 10%))	14.92%				
Project B					
Net cash flow	($5,000)	$1,000	$1,000	$2,000	$3,000
MIRR (=MIRR(B7:F7, 10%, 10%))	11.55%				

The 10% used in the above calculation is the cost of capital. Like NPV, MIRR depends on the cost of capital while computing the returns.

Below is the MIRR for the other example:

	Years			
	0	1	2	3
Net cash flow	($135,000)	$46,000	$46,000	$106,000
MIRR (@10% cost of capital)	16.28%			

If we take a cost of capital of 20% then we get:

	Years			
	0	1	2	3
Net cash flow	($135,000)	$46,000	$46,000	$106,000
MIRR (@20% cost of capital)	18.99%			

As we see, the MIRR is less than the cost of capital in the last case. This means that this project should not be taken up as it cannot cover the cost of capital.

MIRR helps in resolving the issue of multiple IRRs. However, we may still get incorrect MIRR for projects with erratic cash flows. Once again, NPV is preferred alternative.

Usage of Capital Budgeting Methods

The above described capital budgeting methods provide different information related to capital projects. Payback and discounted payback provide information about the liquidity and risk involved in a project (projects with longer payback have higher risks). NPV helps decide whether to accept a project or not. IRR and MIRR give an idea of the safety margin that the project's returns provide above the cost of capital.

In reality, companies use a combination of all the above methods in making a capital budgeting decision.

Solved Examples

4.1 ABC Inc. is planning a new project. It requires an equipment purchase for $10 million and it will also need an initial increase in working capital of $2 million. What is the project's initial investment outlay?

Solution:

The initial investment outlay is the amount of money invested in fixed assets and increase in working capital at the beginning of the project. In the above case the total investment at the beginning of the project is $10 million + $2 million = $12 million. This is the project's initial investment outlay.

4.2 XYZ Inc. is thinking of buying new equipment for its Production department for increasing its work efficiency. The equipment's base cost is $200,000 and would cost another $10,000 for installation. This equipment would be depreciated over 3 years with the depreciation rates being 33%, 45% and 15% over the 3 years. The equipment can be sold for $30,000 after 3 years. The equipment would not generate any additional revenue but save $70,000 every year in before-tax operating costs. There will be an increase in operating working capital by $5,000 in the beginning and the amount will be recovered in the terminal year. The company marginal income tax rate is 40%.

a) **Calculate net cash flows for Year 0.**

b) **What are the net cash flows in Years 1, 2 and 3?**

c) **What are the terminal year cash flows?**

d) **If the cost of capital is 10%, should the equipment be bought?**

Solution:

a) In Year 0, the cash flows are the ones that are expended at the beginning of the project. The following expenses will be relevant:

Equipment cost = $200,000

Installation cost = $10,000

Increase in operating working capital = $5,000

Total cash outflow in Year 0 = $215,000

b) The depreciation schedule for the equipment (including installation cost) is as shown below:

	Years			Cumulative
	1	2	3	Depreciation
Depreciation percentage	33%	45%	15%	
Depreciation (on $210,000)	$69,300	$94,500	$31,500	$195,300
Ending Book Value	$140,700	$46,200	$14,700	

The net cash flows for Year 1, 2 and 3 are as shown below:

	Years		
	1	2	3
Operating cash flows over life of project			
Cost savings	$70,000	$70,000	$70,000
Depreciation (on $210,000)	($69,300)	($94,500)	($31,500)
Operating income (EBIT)	$700	($24,500)	$38,500
Taxes (@ 40%)	($280)	$9,800	($15,400)
Net Operating Profit After Tax (NOPAT)	$420	($14,700)	$23,100
Add back Depreciation	$69,300	$94,500	$31,500
Operating (net) cash flow	$69,720	$79,800	$54,600

c) The terminal year (Year 3) cash flow includes the salvage value received for the equipment and the return of operating working capital. The salvage of $30,000 is greater than the remaining book value of $14,700. Hence, capital gains tax would also have to be paid as shown below:

Terminal year cash flows	
Salvage value of equipment	$30,000
Capital gains tax (@40%)	($6,120)
Return of operating working capital	$5,000
Net cash flow	$28,880

d) In order to decide whether to buy the new equipment we need to find the NPV of this project. If NPV > 0 then the project is worth investing in. Otherwise, it is not. Below sheet shows all the cash flows for this project over 3 years along with the NPV:

		Years		
	0	1	2	3
Initial investment outlay				
Equipment cost	($200,000)			
Installation cost	($10,000)			
Increase in operating working capital	($5,000)			
Total initial investment outlay	($215,000)			
Operating cash flows over life of project				
Cost savings		$70,000	$70,000	$70,000
Depreciation (on $210,000)		($69,300)	($94,500)	($31,500)
Operating income (EBIT)		$700	($24,500)	$38,500
Taxes (@ 40%)		($280)	$9,800	($15,400)
Net Operating Profit After Tax (NOPAT)		$420	($14,700)	$23,100
Add back Depreciation		$69,300	$94,500	$31,500
Operating (net) cash flow		$69,720	$79,800	$54,600
Terminal year cash flow				
Salvage value of equipment				$30,000
Capital gains tax (@40%)				($6,120)
Return of operating working capital				$5,000
Total terminal cash flow				$28,880
Net cash flow	($215,000)	$69,720	$79,800	$83,480
Cost of capital	10%			
NPV	-22,948			

As NPV < 0, the equipment should not be bought.

4.3 Project Z has a cost of $50,000 and its net cash flow per year is $15,000 for 5 years. The cost of capital is 11%. What is the project's payback period?

Solution:

Below is the net cash flow over 8 years along with the cumulative net cash flow:

	Years					
	0	**1**	**2**	**3**	**4**	**5**
Net cash flow	($50,000)	$15,000	$15,000	$15,000	$15,000	$15,000
Cumulative Net cash flow	($50,000)	($35,000)	($20,000)	($5,000)	$10,000	$25,000

Payback period

= 3 + ($5,000/$15,000)

= 3.33 years

4.4 Calculate the above project's discounted payback period and IRR.

Solution:

Discounted payback period:

	Years					
	0	**1**	**2**	**3**	**4**	**5**
Net cash flow	($50,000)	$15,000	$15,000	$15,000	$15,000	$15,000
Discounted net cash flow	($50,000)	$13,514	$12,174	$10,968	$9,881	$8,902
Cumulative Discounted net cash flow	($50,000)	($36,486)	($24,312)	($13,344)	($3,463)	$5,438

Discounted payback period

= 4 + ($3,463/$8,902)

= 4.39

IRR:

	Years					
	0	**1**	**2**	**3**	**4**	**5**
Net cash flow	($50,000)	$15,000	$15,000	$15,000	$15,000	$15,000
IRR	15.24%					

Practice Exercise

4.1 ABC Inc. is faced with an investment proposal. The project in that proposal has the following yearly details:

Year	Net Income	Depreciation rates
1	$50,000	33%
2	$60,000	45%
3	$70,000	15%
4	$60,000	7%

Assume no interest expense and no income tax. There is an initial investment of $100,000 in equipment purchase with an estimated salvage value of $15,000. Company will also need to take an additional operating working capital of $5,000 which will be recovered in year 4. The cost of capital for the project is 12%. Calculate the project's NPV and IRR.

4.2 XYZ Inc. is planning development of a new product. The following information is available about the new product:

a) The product will last 4 years

b) Upfront cost for purchase of new production line will be $300 million with a salvage value at the end of 4 years of $50 million

c) Depreciation will be over 4-year straight-line basis

d) Additional inventory of $60 million will be needed at the beginning of the project. Accounts payable will also rise by $10 million at the beginning. The net operating working capital is recovered at the end of 4 years.

e) Sales per year are estimated to be $200 million over the 4 year period

f) Operating costs per year, excluding depreciation, will be $100 million

g) Marginal tax rate is 40%

h) Project's cost of capital (WACC) is 10%

Calculate the project's NPV.

4.3 Two projects are being considered by a company. They are mutually exclusive and have the following cash flows:

Year	Project A	Project B
0	-$50,000	-$50,000
1	$15,625	$0
2	$15,625	$0
3	$15,625	$0
4	$15,625	$0
5	$15,625	$99,500

If the required rate of return is 10%, which project should be chosen and why?

4.4 ZZZ Inc. has two independent projects it can invest in. The company has a policy to recover all costs within 3 years. It uses the discounted payback method to assess projects with a discount rate (cost of capital) of 10%. The following cash flows are estimated for the two projects:

Year	Project A	Project B
0	-$100,000	-$80,000
1	$40,000	$50,000
2	$40,000	$20,000
3	$40,000	$30,000
4	$30,000	$0

Which project(s) should the company invest in?

This page is intentionally left blank

Chapter **5**

Working Capital Management

The term," working capital", can have several different meanings. One common aspect of all these is that it refers to current assets and liabilities. Below are the most commonly used terms related to working capital:

Working Capital (or Gross Working Capital)

This term simply refers to the current assets of a company, like inventory, accounts receivable, cash, marketable securities etc.

Net Working Capital

The difference between current assets and current liabilities is termed as net working capital.

Net Operating Working Capital

This is the current assets minus non-interest bearing current liabilities. The interest bearing current liabilities signify the money borrowed by the company as a short-term loan. Non-interest bearing current liabilities are the ones that come out of regular business, like accounts payable and accruals.

Working capital is required by every company as it provides the cash needed to pay for loan interests and other day-to-day operations of the company. Depending upon the kind of business that a company is in, it decides how much working capital to carry. Too much working capital leads to reduction in profitability and too less could lead to bankruptcy.

In the sections below we see how a company calculates how much working capital it needs to carry.

Cash Conversion Cycle

The length of time a dollar is tied up in current assets is called the cash conversion cycle. By calculating this length, a company gets an idea of how much working capital it would need and also how the company can improve its operations to reduce the length of this cycle.

Companies buy raw materials, convert them into finished products and sell them. This is the business cycle of a typical company. Companies also get a credit period to pay for their raw materials, called Payables Deferral Period. Similarly, companies also extend credit to their customers, called DSO (this term was seen in chapter 2 earlier) or Receivables Collection Period. When we draw these on a time scale, we get the following:

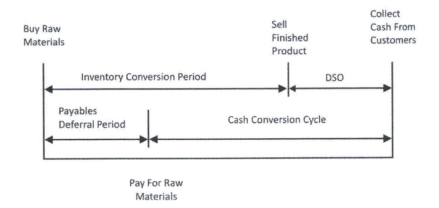

As seen above, the Cash Conversion Cycle is the amount of time taken from the time money is paid for the raw materials to the time money is collected from customers for finished product. The below formula gives this relationship:

Cash Conversion Cycle (CCC) = Inventory Conversion Period + DSO – Payables Deferral Period

In order to reduce the required working capital, a company needs to reduce the CCC. This can be achieved either by reducing the inventory conversion period, shortening the DSO or increasing the payables deferral period. These are the 3 levers that a company has to control the CCC. Below is an example:

If a company takes 50 days to manufacture a product, gives 30 days credit to its customers and gets 20 days to make payments to its suppliers, then the CCC is given as:

CCC = 50 + 30 - 20 = 60 days

If the company manages to reduce its manufacturing lead time to 40 days, make collections from customers in 25 days and extend the credit period offered by its suppliers to 25 days, then the CCC becomes:

CCC = 40 + 25 − 25 = 40 days

In the above example, the company used all 3 levers to reduce its cash conversion cycle by 20 days. This means that the company would require less amount of working capital in its business, thereby, improving its profitability.

A company's inventory conversion period can be calculated as below:

Inventory Conversion Period = Inventory/Sales per day

For example, if a company is carrying an inventory worth $100,000 and it has annual sales of $1 million, then inventory conversion period is:

Inventory Conversion Period = $100,000/($1 million/365) = 36.5 days

DSO is calculated using the below formula:

DSO = Accounts receivable/Sales per day

If a company has $50,000 as accounts receivable and annual sales of $1 million, then its DSO is:

DSO = $50,000/($1 million/365) = 18.25 days

Payables deferral period is given as:

Payables deferral period = Accounts payable/Cost of goods sold per day

If a company has $20,000 in accounts payable and buys raw materials worth $500,000 per year, its payables deferral period is:

Payables deferral period = $20,000/($500,000/365) = 14.6 days

Finally, the CCC will be:

CCC = 36.5 + 18.25 − 14.6 = 40.15 days

Current Asset Investment Policies

Companies have their own policies on how much current assets they would like to have. In general these policies can be divided into three types:

a) **Restricted policy** – Holding current assets is minimized. This is a policy where the company maintains very low amount of current assets. This helps in parking more money in fixed assets, thereby, increasing profitability. However, the company also risks being short of cash to pay its debtors that could lead to bankruptcy.

b) **Relaxed policy** – The company is liberal in holding current assets. Holding far too many current assets could reduce the returns to stockholders but allows the company to pay off its cash obligations with ease.

c) **Moderate policy** – This is between restricted and relaxed policies. This policy allows managers to hold current assets that are required for their business activities without too many restrictions but at the same time does not give a free hand like in a relaxed policy. This policy tries to remove the deficiencies of both, a restricted policy and a relaxed policy, by striking a balance between profitability and risk of bankruptcy.

Current Asset Financing Approaches

In the previous sections we saw why a company needs current assets and how much current assets are appropriate. Now in the next few sections we shall see the financing options available with a company to raise current assets and their comparison.

Companies carry two kinds of assets – fixed and current. Current assets can be further broken up into permanent and temporary. The permanent current assets are those that company needs for a minimum, irrespective of the business cycle. For example, a company needs to carry a certain minimum amount of inventory even during off-peak period and it will also have some amount of accounts receivable. These add up to current assets that are relatively permanent in nature. During peak season the company's sales pick-up and that would mean greater amount of inventory and accounts receivable. These current assets occur only during peak seasons and hence are termed as temporary current assets.

There are three kinds of approaches that companies adopt in financing their assets. They are:

Maturity Matching Approach

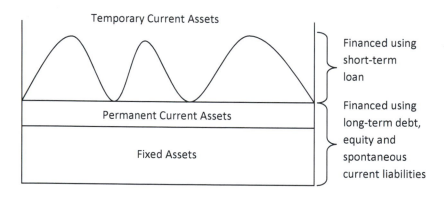

In this approach a company finances its fixed and permanent current assets through long-term capital and spontaneous liabilities (whose maturity matches with that of the current assets).

Spontaneous liabilities are those liabilities that increase or decrease spontaneously with the level of sales, like accounts payable and accrued liabilities. For example, if the company needs $10 million for investing in fixed assets and $1 million in permanent current assets, it will raise $11 million through long-term debt, equity, or automatically by increased accounts payable. All temporary current assets are financed through short-term loans whose period matches with that of the temporary current assets. For example, if a company needs $2 million on extra inventory and accounts receivable during peak season that is expected to last 2 months, then the company will finance it through a $2 million short-term bank loan. Below diagram shows this approach:

Aggressive Approach

Companies following an aggressive approach finance a part of their permanent current assets through short-term loans. The fixed assets are financed through long-term debt and equity as in the maturity matching approach and the temporary current assets through short-term loans. This is a relatively risky approach as the company needs to look for short-term finance on an ongoing basis for its permanent current assets. Below diagram shows this approach:

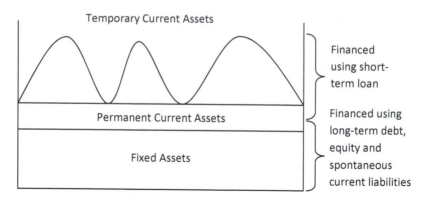

Conservative Approach

This approach is the opposite of the aggressive approach. The company finances most of its temporary current assets using long-term debt and equity. It uses very little short-term financing for some part of the temporary current assets only. This is the least risky approach and is as shown below:

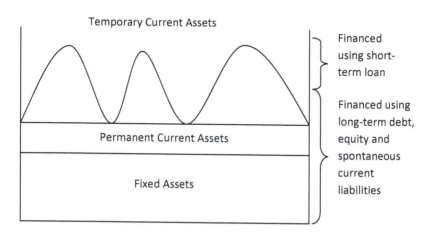

There are reasons why companies follow different approaches described above. The main reason is the risk taking appetite of the company's management. The risk comes from the pros and cons of short-term financing as below:

Advantages of Short-term Financing

a) Short-term finance can be arranged more quickly than long-term debt.

b) Banks generally don't put too many restrictions when extending short-term loans. Whereas, long-term loan agreements could put constraints on the company in terms of its operations.

c) Short-term debt involves lower risk to the bank and hence it is cheaper.

Disadvantages of Short-term Financing

a) By taking long-term loans companies lock themselves into an interest rate for a long period. With short-term financing interest rates would change with every new loan and when rates are going up, this type of loan could be very costly.

b) During liquidity crunch, it might be difficult to raise capital. If a company relies heavily on short-term loans, its operations could be severely affected during such times and could even lead to bankruptcy if enough capital cannot be raised on time.

Short-Term Financing Options

Companies have several ways to raise short-term finance. They are – accrued liabilities, accounts payable (also called trade credit), bank loans, and commercial paper. Each of these is described in the below sections:

Accrued Liabilities

Companies pay their employees on a weekly, bi-weekly, or monthly basis. They also pay their utility bills, income taxes, social security and income tax withheld and sales tax collected after a certain number of days or weeks. These items are shown as accrued liabilities on the company's balance sheet. These can be viewed as "free" short-term financing options as there is no interest charge on these items. Although companies can use these as a way for short-term financing, they have little control over their amount or timing.

Accounts Payable (Trade Credit)

When companies buy raw materials from their suppliers, they receive a credit period. This is a normal practice prevalent in most industries. This form of credit is shown in a company's balance sheet as Accounts Payable. It is also called Trade Credit as it comes from a trading transaction. The company is allowed to use these funds for the period of the credit and it acts as a short-term financing option. This option generally gives the largest amount of short-term financing for most companies. It is also a "spontaneous" form of financing as it increases or decreases in proportion to the company's sales.

However, most suppliers offer a discount if a part of the credit is not utilized. For example, if a supplier says that the payment terms are 2/10, net 30, it means that a 2% discount is available if the payment is made within 10 days else, the entire payment is to be paid in 30 days. It means that if a company is taking the entire credit period, then it is losing on the discount and consequently incurring a cost. In the above case, the company is giving up a 2% discount by taking an extra credit period of 20 days. Assume that the amount to be paid is $100. If the company pays by the 10th day then it needs to pay only $98. If it decides to pay by the 30thday, then it has to pay the entire amount of $100. This means that the company is paying $2 extra on a $98 item over 20 days (difference between 30 days and 10 days).The formula used to calculate the cost of this credit is given below:

Cost of trade credit = ($2/$98) x (365/20) = 37.24%

As seen above, the cost of trade credit can be very high and hence, raising short-term finance using other means might be preferable.

Bank Loans

Commercial banks offer short-term loans to companies based on their credit score. These loans are tailored to be of different maturities and amounts. Banks may also ask for collaterals against loans. Interest rate offered depends upon the credit score of the company and its relationship with the bank. Banks also offer informal lines of credit to avoid negotiating a short-term loan when it is needed. This is like a pre-approved loan upto a certain amount. Banks also get into revolving credit agreements, wherein they promise to extend a short-term loan up to a certain amount to the company at a certain interest rate. Due to this commitment, the company would need to pay an annual commitment fee to the bank.

Companies may need to pay interest and principal back on a monthly, quarterly, or yearly basis. Depending upon the payment frequency, the effective rate of interest will be different. If the company pays in monthly instalments, then its effective rate will be higher than if it pays once a year. So, if two companies have taken a loan at 10% interest rate but one pays monthly interest, whereas, the other pays once a year, the prior company's effective rate of interest will be higher even though both the companies have taken loan at the same rate.

Lets' consider an example. A company is planning to take a bank loan of $100,000 for 1 year. It has two options – an interest rate of 6% with a single interest payment at the end of the year, and an interest rate of 5.9% with interest payments every month. Principle amount has to be returned at the end of 1 year in both cases. The effective interest rate in these two cases is to be calculated using the equation below:

Effective Annual Rate (EAR) = $(1 + (r/m))^m - 1$

Where, r is the rate of interest, and m is the number of compounding periods per year

In the first case, interest is to be paid only once at the end of 1 year. Its EAR is given as:

$EAR_1 = (1 + (6\%/1))^1 - 1 = (1 + 0.06) - 1$

$= 0.06$ or 6%

In the second case, interest is to be paid 12 times through the year. Its EAR is given as:

$EAR_2 = (1 + (5.9\%/12))^{12} - 1 = (1 + 0.0049)^{12} - 1 = 1.0606 - 1$

$= 0.0606$ or 6.06%

The above example shows how the "nominal" interest rate of 5.9% gives a higher "effective" interest rate when payment is to be made over 12 equal instalments.

Commercial Paper

Large companies with strong balance sheets are allowed to issue unsecured promissory notes called Commercial Paper. These allow the company to borrow money for a short duration (less than 1 year) from other companies, insurance companies, pension funds, money market mutual funds, and from banks. Interest rate is generally a little higher than the T-bill rate. T-bill is a treasury bill issued by the government and is actively traded on the exchange.

Solved Examples

5.1 ABC Inc. has an inventory conversion period of 80 days, receivables collection period of 20 days, and payables deferral period of 25 days.

a) **Calculate the company's cash conversion cycle.**

b) **If the company has annual sales of $5 million, all of them on credit, what is the level of company's accounts receivable?**

c) **What is the company's inventory turnover?**

Solution:

a) CCC = Inventory conversion period + Receivables collection period (DSO) – Payables deferral period

   CCC = 80 + 20 – 25 = 75 days

b) Receivables collection period/DSO = Accounts receivable/Sales per day

   Therefore,

   Accounts receivable = DSO x Sales per day

   = 20 x ($5 million/365) = $273,972.60

c) Inventory conversion period = Inventory/Sales per day

   Therefore,

   Inventory = Inventory conversion period x Sales per day

   = 80 x ($5 million/365) = $1,095,890.41

   Inventory turnover = Sales/Inventory

   = $5 million/$1,095,890.41 = 4.56

5.2 XYZ Inc. is establishing its current assets policy. Its fixed assets are $500,000 and it wants to have a 50% debt-to-assets ratio. It is considering three alternatives for current assets – 40, 50 and 60% of sales. The company's EBIT is expected to be 20% of $5 million sales. It has a 40% effective tax rate and 12% interest rate on all debt. What is the expected ROE under each alternative?

Solution:

Fixed assets = $500,000

Debt-to-assets ratio = Total liabilities/Total assets = 0.5

Sales = $5 million

EBIT = $5 million x 0.2 = $1 million

Alternative 1 (Current Assets = 40% of Sales)

Current Assets = $5 million x 0.4 = $2 million

Total Assets = $500,000 + $2 million = $2.5 million

Total Liabilities = $2.5 million x 0.5 = $1.25 million

Total Equity = $2.5 million - $1.25 million = $1.25 million

Alternative 2 (Current Assets = 50% of Sales)

Current Assets = $5 million x 0.5 = $2.5 million

Total Assets = $500,000 + $2.5 million = $3 million

Total Liabilities = $3 million x 0.5 = $1.5 million

Total Equity = $3 million - $1.5 million = $1.5 million

Alternative 3 (Current Assets = 60% of Sales)

Current Assets = $5 million x 0.6 = $3 million

Total Assets = $500,000 + $3 million = $3.5 million

Total Liabilities = $3.5 million x 0.5 = $1.75 million

Total Equity = $3.5million - $1.75 million = $1.75 million

The below sheet shows the rest of the calculations for each alternative:

	Alternative 1	Alternative 2	Alternative 3
Current Assets	$2,000,000	$2,500,000	$3,000,000
Fixed Assets	$500,000	$500,000	$500,000
Total Assets	$2,500,000	$3,000,000	$3,500,000
Debt (Liabilities)	$1,250,000	$1,500,000	$1,750,000
Equity	$1,250,000	$1,500,000	$1,750,000
Total Liabilities & Equity	$2,500,000	$3,000,000	$3,500,000
Sales	$5,000,000	$5,000,000	$5,000,000
EBIT	$1,000,000	$1,000,000	$1,000,000
Interest Expense	$150,000	$180,000	$210,000
PBT	$850,000	$820,000	$790,000
Income Tax Expense	$340,000	$328,000	$316,000
Net Income	$510,000	$492,000	$474,000
ROE	40.80%	32.80%	27.09%

5.3 A wholesaler gives trade credit to its retailers. The terms of credit are 3/15, net 45. However, one of the retailers consistently delays payments to 60 days. What is the cost of trade credit if the retailer pays as per the terms? What is the cost of credit that the retailer is enjoying by paying late?

Solution:

When paying on time, the retailer has the following cost of trade credit:

Cost of trade credit

= (3/97) x (365/30)

= 37.63%

When stretching payments, the retailer has the following cost of trade credit:

Cost of trade credit

= (3/97) x (365/45)

= 25.09%

5.4 AAA Inc. has taken a bank loan to finance its short-term requirements. The loan is for $20,000 at a nominal rate of interest of 10%. Simple interest is to be paid on a monthly basis. Assuming a 365-day year, calculate the company's interest cost in the first month – January.

Solution:

Rate of interest = 10%

Total interest for the year = $20,000 x (10/100) = $2,000

Interest per day = $2,000/365 = $5.4795

Interest for month of January

= $5.4795 x 31

= $169.863

Practice Exercise

5.1 ABC Inc. has revenue of $50,735,000 by keeping raw materials average worth $15,012,000. The payments pending from customers on an average is $10,008,000. Credit period is 40 days, but they don't utilize this time, and pay in 30 days only. They have now decided to utilize the complete credit period. For the same sales, if the raw materials in stock go down by $1,946,000 and pending receipts are reduced by $1,946,000, what will be the change in the cash conversion cycle? (Assume a 365-day year)

5.2 XYZ Inc. is trying to decide its strategy for current managing assets. The firm has $100,000 worth of fixed assets, annual sales of $400,000, and debt is 50% of the company's assets. The firm's interest expense is 10% and the firm's tax rate is 40%. Operating profit stand at $36,000. If they follow a liberal policy, current assets will be 25% of sales. Under a strict policy, current assets will be 15% of sales. What is the difference in the expected ROEs between the different policies?

5.3 Calculate the nominal cost of trade credit in the below situations:
a) 1/15, net 20
b) b) 2/15, net 40
c) 2/10, net 60

This page is intentionally left blank

Chapter 6

Capital Structure

Companies raise capital using two major ways – equity and debt. The prior is generally costlier than the latter but the latter is riskier. The target capital structure of a company is, hence, a trade-off between these two means of raising capital.

Debt

Debt is generally cheaper for most firms as interest paid on debt is tax deductible. However, the effective tax rates of companies are different due to their depreciation expenses, tax loss carry-forwards, and interest on current debt. Hence, the tax benefit is also different for different firms. If a company is unable to pay interest on its debt then the company is led to bankruptcy. Hence, taking on more debt makes the company riskier. But increasing more debt also increases the returns to its common stockholders if the company is able to earn more than the interest it pays on debt.

Every company needs to manage these two factors and decide upon the best ratio of debt and equity that maximizes shareholder wealth. Depending upon the amount of debt used by a company, there are two types of risks called Business risk and Financial risk.

Business Risk

The risk that is inherent in a company's business is called its business risk. This is the risk that a company faces when it has no debt funding. Hence, the factors that determine this risk are the industry in which the company operates, its market demand size, company's business strategy, exposure to foreign exchange etc. All these are operational risks.

Financial Risk

When a company takes on debt funding, it adds a new risk called financial risk. Hence, financial risk is the increase in risk borne by common stockholders of the company that results from use of debt funding (also called financial leverage). The higher the financial leverage, higher is the risk. The main reason for this increased risk is because if the company is unable to pay the interest on its debts, it could go bankrupt. The main reason why companies go for debt is because it provides a cheaper source of funding as interest expense reduces the company's tax liability. However, as the company takes on more debt, its risk increases and so does the rate of interest on its debt. This is because banks and other lenders charge a higher interest rate as they are taking a higher amount of risk by lending to a company with higher leverage. A typical applicable interest rate chart may look like the one below:

Amount of Debt	Debt/Assets Ratio	Interest Rate (cost of debt, k_d)
$10,000	10%	7.5%
$20,000	20%	8.0%
$30,000	30%	8.5%
$40,000	40%	9.25%
$50,000	50%	10.0%
$60,000	60%	11.5%

As seen in the above table, there is a steep rise in the interest rate on debt when the company is highly leveraged. Whether this is beneficial for the common stockholders or not depends on whether the increased leverage adds greater value to the company by increasing its stock price. In the next section we shall see how a company determines how much debt funding it should take.

Optimal Capital Structure

Any company's objective is to maximize its stock price. When a company with no debt starts on taking debt funding, its risk increases but up to a certain point, its stock price also increases as it has a higher potential to increase returns to the shareholders. But beyond a certain level, the risk becomes so high that any further debt will bring down the stock price. Hence, companies need to strike a balance between leverage and risk.

It is difficult to calculate a company's stock price based on different levels of debt funding. However, when a company's stock price is highest, its cost of capital (WACC) is lowest. This can be used to determine the optimal capital structure of the company. WACC is given as below (assuming no preferred stock):

$$WACC = w_d k_d (1 - T) + w_s k_s$$

Let's say that the tax rate, T = 40%

Cost of common stock, $k_s = k_{RF} + (k_M - k_{RF}) \times b_i$

Let's say

Risk-free return, $k_{RF} = 6\%$

Market return, $k_M = 12\%$

b_i will change based on the amount of debt taken by the company. As more debt is taken, the beta will increase. Let's consider the values of beta as per the below table:

Debt/Assets	Cost of debt, k_d	Beta, b_i *	Cost of equity, k_s **	WACC ***
0%	-	1.50	15.00%	15.00%
10%	7.5%	1.60	15.60%	14.49%
20%	8.0%	1.73	16.38%	14.06%
30%	8.5%	1.89	17.34%	13.67%
40%	9.25%	2.10	18.60%	13.38%
50%	10.0%	2.40	20.40%	13.20%
60%	11.5%	2.85	23.10%	13.38%

-* Calculation of beta is as per Hamada's equation that will be seen in the next section

-** $k_s = k_{RF} + (k_M - k_{RF}) \times b_i$

-*** $WACC = w_d k_d (1 - T) + w_s k_s$, assuming a tax rate of 40%

As seen from the above table, the WACC reduces as more debt is taken until the debt reaches 50% of total assets. After that the WACC starts increasing as the risk grows further. Hence, the company's optimal capital structure is when debt is 50% of assets. If the company maintains this capital structure, it can expect its stock price to be higher than any other capital structure if all other factors are kept constant.

Hamada Equation

The calculation of beta in the previous section was done using the Hamada Equation. It is as given below:

$b = b_u \times [1 + (1 - T) \times (D/E)]$

where, b is the beta co-efficient

b_u is the unlevered beta co-efficient (beta when no debt funding is taken)

T is the tax rate

(D/E) is the debt-to-equity ratio

When a company does not take any debt funding, its risk is lowest and hence the beta (b_u) is the lowest. Let's say the unlevered beta of the company is 1.5 and its debt-to-assets ratio is 10%. This means that if assets are worth $100, then debt is worth $10. This means that equity will be worth $90 (assets = debt + equity). Hence, its debt-to-equity ratio will be 11.11%. Then, to calculate its beta we do the following:

$b = 1.5 \times [1 + (1 - 0.4) \times 0.111] = 1.5 \times 1.067 = 1.60$

Capital Structure Theories

There are two important theories related to a company's capital structure. They are given below:

Trade-Off Theory

Due to the tax deduction available on interest paid on debt, companies prefer to use debt funding. If there were no other considerations or risks, this would lead to a 100% debt funding. However, as the debt increases, so does the risk of the company not being able to pay its interest on debt, and hence the chance of bankruptcy. Hence, there is a trade-off between tax deduction and the cost of bankruptcy. As seen in the previous section, this trade-off will be seen in the WACC and the stock price of the company. This trade-off will determine the company's optimal capital structure. It goes as per the below diagram:

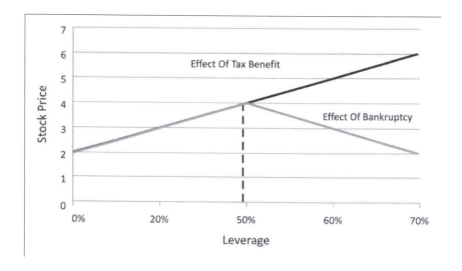

As seen above, as the company takes on more debt (higher leverage), its stock price increases due to the effect of tax benefit. However, the effect of bankruptcy pulls the stock price down after an increase in leverage beyond a certain amount. The combined effect is that the stock price goes up and after reaching its highest point comes down. The point at which it is highest is where the company has an optimal capital structure.

Signaling Theory

Managers in companies have certain information about the firm that stockholders do not have. This is called "asymmetric information". Due to this, investors are unable to predict the company's future as good as its managers can. Due to this information asymmetry, stockholders follow certain signals given by the company. One such signal is issue of new common equity. Whenever a company goes for a new issue of common stock, it is viewed as a negative signal by existing stockholders and the stock price goes down. Another signal is the issue of new debt funding by a company. Debt funding is seen as a positive signal by existing stockholders and the stock prices generally rise when new debt is issued.

The above signals have been proved through empirical studies and hence companies generally keep a reserve borrowing capacity. This means that companies take on less debt than their optimal capital structure so that they can borrow in future when there are good investment opportunities. Hence, companies might use lower debt than what is being suggested by the trade-off theory above.

Solved Examples

6.1 ABC Inc. is trying to determine its optimal capital structure. The company believes that the optimal structure lies between 10% and 40% debt. The below projections of the stock price at different levels of debt is available.

Debt-to-assets ratio	Projected stock price
10%	$20
20%	$22.50
30%	$24.24
40%	$23.75

Assuming that the company uses only common stock and debt, what is the company's optimal capital structure? At what debt-to-assets ratio is the company's WACC minimum?

Solution:

The company should aim to maximize its stock price. For it to achieve this objective, it needs to select a debt-to-assets ratio of 30%, as it gives the maximum projected stock price.

The company's WACC is at a minimum at the point where its projected stock price is highest. Hence, the WACC is at a minimum at a debt-to-assets ratio of 30%.

6.2 XYZ Inc. has total assets of $5 million. The company has taken $1 million as debt and another $4 million in the form of common equity. If the company's beta is currently 1.5 and its tax rate is 40%, what is the company's unlevered beta, b_u?

Solution:

As per Hamada equation, $b = b_u \times [1 + (1 - T) \times (D/E)]$

Hence, unlevered beta, b_u

$= b/[1 + (1 - T) \times (D/E)]$

$= 1.5/[1 + (1 - 0.4) \times (\$1/\$4)]$

$= 1.5/1.15 = 1.304$

6.3 ZZZ Inc. wants to determine its optimal capital structure. It does not have any preferred stock. It has collected information at different levels of debt:

Debt-to-assets ratio (w_d)	Equity-to-assets ratio (w_s)	Debt-to-equity ratio (D/E)	Cost of debt (k_d)
0	1.0	0	5.5%
0.10	0.90	0.11	6.0%
0.20	0.80	0.25	7.0%
0.30	0.70	0.43	8.25%
0.40	0.60	0.67	10.0%

The risk-free rate is 5%, tax rate is 40%, and the average market return is 12%. Company's unlevered beta is 1.1. Determine the company's optimal capital structure.

Solution:

Optimal capital structure is the one at which the WACC is minimum. Hence, we need to compute the WACC. Weight of debt, weight of equity, cost of debt and tax rate are given. We need to calculate the cost of equity for the various debt-to-assets ratios as the beta would change for each capital structure. Below are the beta calculations:

Debt-to-assets ratio (w_d)	b_u	T	D/E	$b = b_u \times [1 + (1 - T) \times (D/E)]$
0	1.1	40%	0	1.100
0.1	1.1	40%	0.11	1.173
0.2	1.1	40%	0.25	1.265
0.3	1.1	40%	0.43	1.384
0.4	1.1	40%	0.67	1.542

Using the above beta co-efficient, we calculate the cost of equity as below:

Debt-to-assets ratio (w_d)	b	k_{RF}	k_M	$k_s = k_{RF} + (k_M - k_{RF}) \times b_i$
0	1.1	5%	12%	12.70%
0.1	1.173	5%	12%	13.21%
0.2	1.265	5%	12%	13.86%
0.3	1.384	5%	12%	14.69%
0.4	1.542	5%	12%	15.79%

Finally, the WACC is calculated using the above values as below:

w_d	k_d	w_s	k_s	T	WACC = $w_d k_d (1 - T) + w_s k_s$
0	5.50%	1.0	12.70%	40%	12.70%
0.1	6.00%	0.9	13.21%	40%	12.25%
0.2	7.00%	0.8	13.86%	40%	11.93%
0.3	8.25%	0.7	14.69%	40%	11.77%
0.4	10.00%	0.6	15.79%	40%	11.87%

As seen from the above table, the company's WACC is at a minimum when its debt-to-assets ratio is 0.3. Hence, the company should take on 30% debt and 70% common equity as its optimal capital structure.

Practice Exercise

6.1 ABC Inc. has a capital structure of 25% debt and 75% equity. The company wants to see the effect of changing it to 50% debt and 50% equity. The risk free return is given as 5% and the average market return is 11%. The company's applicable tax rate is 40% and its current cost of equity is 14%. What will be the company's cost of equity with the new capital structure?

6.2 Following information is available regarding XYZ Inc.:

Total assets:	$3,000 million
EBIT:	$800 million
Interest expense:	$0
Net Income:	$480 million
Share price:	$32
Tax rate:	40%
Debt ratio:	0
WACC:	10%
EPS	$3.20

The company pays out all its earnings as dividends. Its stock price can be calculated by dividing earnings per share by the required return on equity, which currently equals the WACC as the company has no debt.

The company believes that if the capital structure consists of 40% debt, then they will be better off. Hence, the company decides to buy-back shares at the current market price by using $1,200 million raised through a bank loan at a before-tax cost of 7%. The repurchase of shares will not have any effect on the

EBIT, but the cost of equity will increase to 11%. What will be the company's estimated stock price after the change in capital structure?

This page is intentionally left blank

Chapter **7**

Distribution to Shareholders

Companies need to distribute the profits they make amongst their common shareholders. They do so in several ways, the most common being through dividends and increase in stock prices. Different companies have different policies for distributing dividends. There are several factors that influence this decision. The following sections describe these factors. Rest of the chapter describes other ways used by companies for profit distribution, namely dividend reinvestment plans (DRIP), stock splits and stock dividends, and stock repurchases. Investors can also sell their shares on the stock exchange to earn capital gains if stock prices have increased since they bought the shares.

Factors in setting Dividend Distribution Policy

Common stockholders can, theoretically, either hold on to their stocks and get dividends from the company or, sell their stocks and get capital gains. If there were no tax effects or transactions charges, then both of these options would be same and, hence, dividend payout ratio (dividend/net income) would be irrelevant. But in reality the tax effects of dividends and capital gains are different. For those in the higher tax bracket, tax on long-term capital gains is generally 20%, whereas, on dividend income, it can be as high as 38.6%. Further, capital gains tax is only to be paid when stock is sold. Due to these reasons, some investors might prefer capital gains to dividends.

On the other hand, retired people might prefer dividend income as they might depend on it to take care of their monthly expenses. They might belong to lower tax bracket and, hence don't need to worry about the tax effect as much as wealthy investors.

Some investors might prefer dividends, irrespective of their tax condition, as they believe in the bird-in-hand theory. These investors value cash dividends more than capital gains as they have already cashed in on the profits and consider it safer. They would like to play safe.

In general, the following broad factors determine investors' preference to dividends:

a) **Investor tax bracket** – those investors in higher tax bracket would prefer capital gains

b) **Investor stage of life** – those who are either retired or close to retirement might prefer high dividend

c) **Investor risk appetite** – those investors willing to take lower risk would prefer higher dividends than capital gains

d) **Timing** – during times of booming stock market, investors might prefer higher capital gains and during a recession/slowdown, prefer higher dividends

It is interesting to note that the same investor might have different preferences during different times. For example, during a bearish stock market, even wealthy investors might prefer to get dividends as opposed to capital gains as they might see the latter more risky.

Companies also differ in their dividend payout ratios. Companies with large number of investment opportunities pay a lower dividend. It is generally seen that the investors who prefer higher dividends flock companies that pay higher dividends and vice versa.

As described above, there is a match between companies and investors, based on their preferences. However, the most important aspect is to maintain the dividend payout. Imagine a company that is known to pay large dividends. It will attract investors with high preference to dividends. If such a company reduces its dividend or stops it, that will cause discontent amongst its current stockholders and there could be high selling of the company's stocks, reducing its stock price. Hence, whatever be the dividend policy, a company needs to keep it stable over time. Stability of dividends is more important than whether the company pays high dividends or not. As long as it pays stable dividends, it will attract and retain like-minded investors.

Whenever a company increases or decreases its dividend payout, it sends a signal to its investors. When the dividend is reduced, it sends a negative signal that the managers of the company think that future prospects of the company are not so good. When dividend is increased, a positive signal is sent that the managers of the company think that the future holds good prospects for the company.

Residual Dividend Model

As discussed in the previous section, stable dividends are expected by investors. Hence, companies need to ensure that they maintain fixed dollar amounts every year, for example, giving $2 dividend every year irrespective of the net income for the year. Companies also give due consideration to rates of inflation and, hence, increase the dividends every year at a constant rate, like 5% every year. This means that the company would pay $2 in the 1st year, $2.10 in the 2nd year, 2.205 in the 3rd year and so on.

Companies plough back their income into their business and whatever is left is paid out as dividends. This is called the residual dividend model. But companies don't always have the same investment opportunities every year. Hence, if they follow residual dividend model every year, then the dividends would vary. This is depicted in the below calculation.

Dividends = Net Income –Retained Earnings

In 1st year, if the company has a Net Income of $50 million and it has investment opportunities worth $20 million, it will give out dividends worth $30 million. In the 2nd year if the earnings remained same but there are more investment opportunities, worth $40 million, then it would pay out $10 million as dividends. Due to instability of dividends, the company might send a negative signal to its stockholders and its stock price might fall.

Hence, companies generally make an estimate of their net income and investment opportunities for the next 5-10 years. They use this average to calculate the dividend payout over these years and try to maintain a stable dividend over these years.

Below are the steps followed by companies that use residual dividend model:

a) Estimate net income and investment opportunities over the next 5-10 years

b) Using the above values, find out the dividend payout ratio over the years

c) Average out the payout ratio over the years on the basis of the above data

Whenever companies do very good business in a particular year, they pay a one-time "extra dividend" on top of the regular dividend, which is kept constant. This ensures that investors do not expect the higher dividend over the years. Hence, companies keep their "regular dividend" low so that they can pay it even in the worst case business scenario.

Dividend Payment Procedures

Dividends are declared by the board of companies on a certain date and actually paid at a later date. The below timeline shows the various dates that have significance related to dividend payments.

Declaration date is when the company declares the dividend payment. Ex-dividend date is the date from which the dividend does not go with the stock. Holder-of-record- date is generally 2 days after the ex-dividend date, when the actual stock ownership

is changed in the company's records. Payment date is when the actual dividend payment is made in cash to the stockholders.

Assume that the company declares a dividend of $5 on 15th Nov and the actual payment is to happen on 15th Jan next year. Then, 15th Nov is called the Declaration date and 15th Jan is called the Payment date. Further consider that the company has decided to keep 15th Dec as the Holder-of-record date, then 13th Dec will be the Ex-dividend date. This means that anybody buying the company's stock on or after 13th Dec will not receive the dividend. The original holder of the stock who sells the stock will be the recipient of the dividend. So the company's stock price should reduce by about $5 at the start of trading on 13th Dec because the buyer will no longer receive the declared dividend of $5.

Dividend Reinvestment Plan (DRIP)

Another way companies distribute profits to investors is via dividend reinvestment plans. Instead of paying out cash dividends, companies buy additional stocks in the investor's name. So after the profit distribution, the investor holds more stocks of the company. This can happen in two ways – by buying "old stock" or already existing stock from the open market, or by buying "new stock" issued by the company. The first option does not provide any extra funding to the company but the second option provides additional funds to the company against issue of new stock. In the first option, the company buys its own stock from the stock market and assigns it in the name of the investor. Hence, the company pays out the amount to the seller of the stock in the stock market against stocks. In the second option, the company retains the profits and issues additional stock of the company to the investor. In this option the number of stocks of the company goes up. Companies often provide these stocks at a discounted rate as they don't need to pay flotation costs. Companies making use of DRIP might also need to constantly assess the needs of their stockholders as they might prefer capital gains to dividend payments and hence, they might be able to reduce their dividend payout ratio instead of reinvesting dividends.

Stock Splits and Stock Dividends

Companies often split shares into multiple parts, like two-for-one. After this split, each common stock of the company would be worth half of what it was before the split. But there is also a signalling effect of stock splits. Markets take stock splits as a result of the company's managers' favourable future assessment of business. This leads to increase in stock prices when stock split is announced. Companies generally do a stock split when each stock is costing outside of the optimal price range, generally said to be $20 - $80. The rationale behind this is that several investors are unable to invest in shares of the company in lots of 100 shares as each share costs too much. With a stock split, more investors will be able to buy, increasing trade volumes of the shares and taking up the stock price. Hence, companies use stock splits to provide higher capital gains to its investors instead of distributing cash dividends.

Stock dividends are similar to stock splits. Companies may give 10% stock dividend to existing stockholders. This means that each stockholder will receive 10 additional shares for each 100 shares held without any extra cost. This also has a signalling effect like stock splits and helps increase the capital gains.

When stock splits and stock dividends are declared, the stock prices rise as investors anticipate higher earnings due to signalling. This price rise is purely due to investor sentiment and has no real bearing to the company's profits. If in the following months the company does not announce increase in earnings, then the stock price might go back to its original level.

Stock Repurchases

Instead of paying out cash dividends companies often buy back shares. These are called treasury stock. The company generally pays a premium when buying back stocks. A stock repurchase also sends positive signal to stockholders about the management's expectations about future prospects. Whether a stock repurchase is more profitable to shareholders who sell their stock back to the company or to remaining stockholders who stay invested depends on the price the company pays for the buy back. If the company pays too high a price for the repurchased stock it will disadvantage the remaining stockholders. The reverse is true if the company pays too low a price for the repurchased stock. Like stock split and stock dividends, stock repurchases also tend to increase the company's stock price due to signalling effect.

Solved Examples

7.1 After a 3-for-1 stock split, ABC Inc. paid a dividend of $0.50 per new share. This is a 10% growth over last year's dividend. What was last year's dividend per share?

Solution:

This year's dividend = $0.50

Dividend growth = 10%

Hence, last year's dividend

= $0.50/1.1 = $0.455

Last year's dividend was on a stock that represents 3 stocks this year. Hence, the dividend per share last year would be 3 times the above value.

Dividend per share last year

= $0.455 x 3 = $1.364

7.2 XYZ Inc. has a target capital structure that contains 40% equity and 60% debt. The company's capital budget next year will be $3 million and its net income is expected to be $2 million. If it follows residual dividend payout policy, what will be its dividend payout ratio next year?

Solution:

As per residual dividend policy:

Dividends = Net Income – Retained Earnings

Retained Earnings are that part of the earnings retained for capital investments.

Total capital investment = $3 million

Total equity part of capital investment

= 40% x $3 million = $1.2 million

Hence, Retained Earnings = $1.2 million

Dividends = $2 million - $1.2 million = $800,000

Dividend payout ratio

= $800,000/$2 million = 40%

7.3 XXX Inc. is considering the below three independent projects, each needing $2 million in investment:

Project A - Cost of capital = 15%   IRR = 22%

Project B - Cost of capital = 12%   IRR = 10%

Project C - Cost of capital = 13%   IRR = 15%

The cost of capital of the projects varies as they are of differing risk levels. The company has an optimal capital structure of 40% debt and 60% equity and it expects to have a net income of $5 million. If the company uses residual dividend model, what will be its dividend payout ratio?

Solution:

The company would only select projects A & C, as only these provide an IRR that is greater than the cost of capital for those projects. As they are independent, both can be selected. Hence, the total investment to be made is $4 million.

Company's capital structure would require the following equity:

Equity requirement = 60% x $4 million = $2.4 million

Using the residual dividend model:

Dividends = $5 million - $2.4 million = $2.6 million

Hence, Dividend payout ratio

= $2.6 million/$5 million = 52%

7.4 YYY Inc. has reported a net income of $2 million for the year. The company has 200,000 shares outstanding and its current stock price is $50 per share.

a) If the company had a 50% dividend payout ratio last year and plans to maintain it, what will be this year's dividend?

b) What will be this year's dividend yield?

c) If the company had reported $1.7 million net income last year, what was its per share dividend (assuming that the number of shares were the same)?

d) Comment on the dollar value of dividends in the two years. Should the company try to maintain the dividend payout ratio or match the dollar value of dividends?

Solution:

a) Dividends = 50% x $2 million = $1 million

b) Dividend yield = Dividend per share/Price per share

     Dividend per share = $1 million/200,000 = $5

     Therefore, Dividend yield = $5/$50 = 10%

c) Dividends last year = 50% x $1.7 million = $850,000

     Therefore, Dividend per share = $850,000/200,000 = $4.25

d) The dividend last year was $4.25 per share. This has been increased this year to $5 per share. This is to keep the same dividend payout ratio. Although this will send positive signals, the company might not be able to continue at this growth rate every year. As investors look for stable dividends, it is best to match the dollar value of per share dividend instead of dividend payout ratio. Any additional amount that the company wants to distribute can be in the form of "extra dividend" in a particular year or through stock repurchases.

Practice Exercise

7.1 XYZ Inc. wants to maintain its capital structure of 70% equity and 30% debt. The expected net income in the year will be $1 million. As per residual dividend model, what should be the company's capital budget, if dividend payout ratio will be 40%?

7.2 AAA Inc. expects to have a net income of $800,000 in the next year. Its optimal capital structure consists of 40% debt and 60% equity. The company would need to make capital investments worth $1.2 million next year. Calculate the company's dividend payout ratio using residual dividend policy.

This page is intentionally left blank

Chapter **8**

Forecasting Financial Statements

Companies forecast their financial statements over the next 5-10 years. This is needed for various reasons, like providing to lenders and banks when taking new debt, setting financial targets for managers and knowing how much money will need to be borrowed in the following years. In this chapter we shall concentrate on the last aspect of knowing how much to borrow during each year.

Forecasted financial statements are called Pro forma financial statements. Percent of Sales method is used in forecasting financial statements and in knowing the amount of funds to be borrowed. There are five steps involved in this method, which are given in the sections below.

Step 1 - Forecast Sales

The first step for any company using Percent of Sales method to forecast financial statements is to do a sales forecast. Companies generally look at the sales growth trend over the last few years to come up with a forecast for the next few years. There can be corrections related to the company's expectations of increase or decrease in demand due to change in market conditions.

The table below shows the sales of a company over the last 5 years. Using this data the company projects its sales for the next year.

Year	Sales (in thousands of dollars)
2007	$1,000
2008	$1,250
2009	$1,550
2010	$2,100
2011	$2,500
2012	$2,800 (projected)

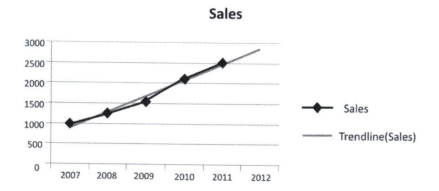

In the above graph, the trend line provides an estimate of the projected sales in 2012. This is assuming that 2012 will have similar market conditions as in the previous 5 years.

Step 2 - Forecast Income Statement

Once the company has projected its sales for the next year, it can forecast the other parts of the income statement, most of which depend on the sales forecast. We will use the below income statement of the company for the current year to forecast its income statement for the next year.

Income statement for 2011	(in thousands of dollars)
Sales	$2,500
Expenses (except depreciation)	$1,875
Depreciation	$200
Operating profit (EBIT)	$425
Interest expense	$100
Profit before Tax (PBT)	$325
Taxes (@30%)	$98
Net Income before preferred dividends	$228
Preferred dividends	$8
Net Income available to common	$220
Common dividends	$100
Addition to retained earnings	$120

We have already forecasted the sales for 2012. Expenses (except depreciation) are generally a percentage of the sales. Depreciation will be based on the basis of the net plant and equipment in 2012. Since we don't have knowledge of the balance sheet for 2012, we shall assume that plant and equipment grow at the same rate in

2012 as does sales. Sales are growing from $2,500 thousand to $2,800 thousand, which is 12% growth. Similarly, we assume that net plant and equipment also grow by 12% and so does the depreciation. We will take the interest expense to be the same as we don't yet know how much more debt we would take on. Taxes are calculated on actual PBT, preferred dividends are also kept constant as we don't know how much more preferred stock will be issued. We will further assume a constant growth of common dividends and will need to assume the same number of common stocks as we don't know how much more would be borrowed by way of common equity. Looking at the past, we take a 10% growth rate in the common dividends. We get the pro forma income statement as below:

	2011 (in 1,000 $)	Forecast basis	2012 (in 1,000 $)
Sales	$2,500	As per Sales forecast	$2,800
Expenses (except depreciation)	$1,875	75% of sales	$2,100
Depreciation	$200	12% growth	$224
Operating profit (EBIT)	$425		$476
Interest expense	$100	Carried as is	$100
Profit before Tax (PBT)	$325		$376
Taxes (@30%)	$98		$113
Net Income before preferred dividends	$228		$263
Preferred dividends	$8	Carried as is	$8
Net Income	$220		$255
Common dividends	$100	10% growth	$110
Addition to retained earnings	$120		$145

Step 3 - Forecast Balance Sheet – 1st Pass

Like the income statement is forecasted in the previous section, in this section we shall forecast the balance sheet. Let's consider the balance sheet of the company in 2011 as below:

Balance sheet for 2011	(in thousands of dollars)
Assets	
Cash and cash equivalents	$50
Accounts receivable	$250
Inventory	$500
Total current assets	$800
Net plant and equipment	$1,500
Total assets	$2,300
Liabilities & Stockholders' equity	
Accounts payable	$300
Accrued liabilities	$100
Notes payable	$500
Total current liabilities	$900
Long-term loans	$500
Total Liabilities	$1,400
Preferred stock	$70
Common stock	$120
Retained earnings	$710
Total liabilities and equity	$2,300

In order to forecast the balance sheet for 2012, we shall assume that the value of all the assets will continue to be the same ratio to sales as it was in 2011. For example, Cash is $50 in 2011 against Sales of $2,500. Hence, Cash is 2% of Sales in 2011. It will continue to be 2% of Sales in 2012 as well. Hence, its value would be 2% of

$2,800, which is $56. Similarly, accounts payable and accrued liabilities will also be carried using the same basis. This is generally true for all current assets and liabilities as these are spontaneous assets and liabilities that increase in proportion to sales.

All the borrowed sources of funds, namely notes payable, long-term loans, preferred stock and common stock are kept the same in the 1st pass. Retained earnings is increased on the basis of addition to retained earnings from the pro forma income statement. Finally, the difference between the total assets and total liabilities & equity will give us a figure called Additional Funds Needed (AFN). These are the additional funds that the company needs to raise in 2012 to sustain its business. In the next step we see how these funds would be raised.

	2011	Forecast basis	2012
	(in 1,000 $)		(in 1,000 $)
Assets			
Cash and cash equivalents	$50	2% of sales	$56
Accounts receivable	$250	10% of sales	$280
Inventory	$500	20% of sales	$560
Total current assets	$800		$896
Net plant and equipment	$1,500	12% growth	$1,680
Total assets	$2,300		$2,576
Liabilities & Stockholders' equity			
Accounts payable	$300	12% of sales	$336
Accrued liabilities	$100	4% of sales	$112
Notes payable	$500	Carried as is	$500
Total current liabilities	$900		$948
Long-term loans	$500	Carried as is	$500
Total Liabilities	$1,400		$1,448
Preferred stock	$70	Carried as is	$70
Common stock	$120	Carried as is	$120
Retained earnings	$710	+$145 from above step	$855
Total liabilities and equity	$2,300		$2,493
AFN			**$83**

We find that $83,000 are needed to finance the additional assets of the company in 2012 to sustain the sales growth.

Step 4 - Raising Additional Funds Needed (AFN)

As seen in the previous step, we need to raise additional funds in 2012 to sustain the increase in sales. This can be done using short-term debt (notes payable), long-term debt, preferred stock or common stock. Let's assume that the company has a certain optimal capital structure in mind using which it decides to keep the preferred stock as it is and raises the additional capital using notes, long-term debt and by issuing new common equity as below.

	Percent	Amount (in 1,000 $)
Notes payable	30%	$25
Long-term loan	30%	$25
Common equity	40%	$33

Step 5 - Forecast Balance Sheet – 2nd Pass

In the previous section we have decided the source of additional funding. This will now be put in the pro forma balance sheet for 2012 to complete it. This is our 2nd pass through the balance sheet.

	2012 (1st pass) (in 1,000 $)	Basis	2012 (2nd pass) (in 1,000 $)
Assets			
Cash and cash equivalents	$56	As is	$56
Accounts receivable	$280	As is	$280
Inventory	$560	As is	$560
Total current assets	$896		$896
Net plant and equipment	$1,680	As is	$1,680
Total assets	$2,576		$2,576
Liabilities & Stockholders' equity			
Accounts payable	$336	As is	$336
Accrued liabilities	$112	As is	$112
Notes payable	$500	+25 (30% of AFN)	$525
Total current liabilities	$948		$973
Long-term loans	$500	+25 (30% of AFN)	$525
Total Liabilities	$1,448		$1,498
Preferred stock	$70	As is	$70
Common stock	$120	+33 (40% of AFN)	$153
Retained earnings	$855	As is	$855
Total liabilities and equity	$2,493		$2,576
AFN	$83		

The above sheet is the pro forma balance sheet for 2012. Now, in reality, we should go back to the pro forma income statement for 2012 to consider the interest effects of additional debt and additional common dividends to new common stockholders. But this would also mean further changes to the balance sheet for 2012 to consider the effects of the changed retained earnings. We can continue going like this to arrive at more accurate pro forma financial statements. However, it is mathematically intensive and adds lesser value compared to the benefit we achieve. The pro forma financial statements that we have prepared above are generally enough to make business decisions. These are pro forma financial statements without financial feedback due to additional funding.

AFN Formula

When pro forma financial statements were prepared in the previous section, the additional funds needed were calculated using them. However, there is also a quick way to find AFN without pro forma financial statement using the formula given below:

AFN = Required increase in assets – Increase in spontaneous liabilities – Increase in retained earnings

Each the component of above equation is explained below:

Required increase in assets – this is the amount by which assets have to increase due to increase in sales. Assets generally increase in proportion to sales. So this is the additional amount of money that the company is going to need. Hence, we find the asset to sales ratio and then estimate this value as below:

(A^*/S_0) x ΔS

Where, A^* - assets that increase directly with sales

S_0 – sales in previous year (2011)

ΔS – change in sales

Increase in spontaneous liabilities – change in all non-interest bearing liabilities that automatically change with a change in sales, like accounts payable increases with increase in sales. This is the amount of funds that the company automatically generates as part of regular business transactions. The formula given below can be used for this:

$(L^*/S_0) \times \Delta S$

Where, L^* - spontaneous liabilities

Increase in retained earnings – this is the additional amount of funding available to the company that has been retained from profits in the previous year. Below formula can be used to calculate this:

MS_1R

Where, M – profit margin of the company

S_1 – sales in projected year (2012)

R – retention ratio of net income. This is the leftover after dividend payout (also given by 1 – payout ratio).

When using the above AFN formula, we get an estimated value of the funds that the company would need to raise next year.

Applying it to the example from the previous section, we get:

Required increase in assets = $(A^*/S_0) \times \Delta S = (\$2,300/\$2,500) \times \$300 = \$276$

Increase in spontaneous liabilities = $(L^*/S_0) \times \Delta S = ((\$300 + \$100)/\$2,500) \times \$300 = \$48$

($300 + $100) above are the 2011 spontaneous liabilities of accounts payable and accrued liabilities

Increase in retained earnings = $MS_1R = (\$220/\$2,500) \times \$2,800 \times (\$120/\$220) = 0.088 \times \$2,800 \times 0.545 = \$134.4$

Hence, AFN = $276 - $48 - $134.4 = $93.6

The value of AFN calculated using the above formula is approximately equal to the one using the pro forma financial statements earlier. The difference is due to the difference in the retention ratio in the two years. However, this is a quick way to calculate the value of AFN and can only be used when the financial ratios of the company would remain the same. If any differences are anticipated then this formula cannot be used.

The AFN formula assumes that all the assets are being utilized at 100% of their capacity. However, if that is not the case, then we first need to calculate the full capacity sales using the current assets before using the AFN formula as below:

Full capacity sales = Actual sales/Percentage capacity utilization of assets

For example, if the assets are being used at 90% of their capacity for generating sales of $2,500, then the same assets can generate additional sales without buying any new assets as below:

Full capacity sales = $2,500/0.9 = $2,778

The figure of $2,778 should then be used as S_0 in the AFN equation to calculate the additional funds needed.

Solved Examples

8.1 ABC Inc.'s sales for 2010 are $4 million and are expected to increase by 25% in 2011. The company has assets worth $6 million in 2010. The company is utilizing its assets at full capacity. The company's current liabilities are worth $500,000, of which $200,000 are accounts payable, $200,000 are notes payable, and $100,000 are accrued liabilities. Company's profit margin is 15% and has a retention ratio of 25%. Calculate the additional funds needed by the company in 2011.

Solution:

$AFN = (A^*/S_0) \times \Delta S - (L^*/S_0) \times \Delta S - MS_1R$

$(A^*/S_0) \times \Delta S = (\$6 \text{ million}/\$4 \text{ million}) \times \$1 \text{ million} = \$1.5 \text{ million}$

$(L^*/S_0) \times \Delta S = ((\$200{,}000 + \$100{,}000)/\$4 \text{ million})) \times \$1 \text{ million}$

$= \$75{,}000$

$MS_1R = 15\% \times \$5 \text{ million} \times 25\% = \$187{,}500$

Therefore, AFN

$= \$1.5 \text{ million} - \$75{,}000 - \$187{,}500$

$= \$1{,}237{,}500$

8.2 XYZ Inc. has $10 million in sales and $5 million fixed assets. The company is currently using 85% of its fixed assets.

a) **How much sales can the company generate using the current fixed assets?**

b) **What is the company's fixed assets/sales ratio?**

c) **In order to increase the sales by 15% how much will the fixed assets need to increase?**

Solution:

a) Company has 15% spare capacity. It can generate the following sales using the same amount of fixed assets:

Sales = $10 million/0.85 = $11.765 million

b) Fixed assets/sales ratio = $5 million/$11.765 million

= 0.425 or 42.5%

c) A 15% increase in sales means

Increase in sales = $10 million + 15% of $10 million
= $11.5 million

As the company's current fixed assets can generate sales worth $11.765 million, there is no need for additional assets to handle sales of $11.5 million.

8.3 Below is AAA Inc.'s income statement for 2010 (in millions of dollars):

Income statement for 2010	
Sales	$1,000
Expenses (except depreciation)	$750
Depreciation	$100
Operating profit (EBIT)	$150
Interest expense	$10
Profit before Tax (PBT)	$140
Taxes (@30%)	$42
Net Income	$98
Dividends	$49
Addition to retained earnings	$49

The company expects to grow sales by 40% in 2011. Its operating expenses will continue to be in the same ratio to sales as in 2010 i.e. (Operating expenses/Sales) will remain constant. Similarly, the tax rate, interest expense, and dividend payout ratio will also continue to be the same.

a) Compute AAA's net income in 2011.

b) What is the growth rate of AAA's dividends?

Solution:

a) As per the data given, following is the pro forma income statement for AAA Inc.:

	2010	Basis	2011
Sales	$1,000	40% growth	$1,400
Expenses (except depreciation)	$750	75% of sales	$1,050
Depreciation	$100	10% of sales	$140
Operating profit (EBIT)	$150		$210
Interest expense	$10	Carried as is	$10
Profit before Tax (PBT)	$140		$200
Taxes (@30%)	$42		$60
Net Income	$98		$140
Dividends	$49	50% dividend payout ratio	$70
Addition to retained earnings	$49		$70

As seen above, the Net Income for 2011 is $140 million. The dividend payout ratio of 50% in 2010 is maintained in 2011 as well.

b) Dividend growth rate

= ($70 - $49)/$49

= 0.4286 or 42.86%

Practice Exercise

8.1 ABC Inc. has the following balance sheet in 2010 (in millions of dollars):

Balance sheet for 2010	(in million of dollars)
Assets	
Cash and cash equivalents	$10
Accounts receivable	$25
Inventory	$40
Total current assets	$75
Net plant and equipment	$75
Total assets	$150
Liabilities & Stockholders' equity	
Accounts payable	$15
Accrued liabilities	$15
Notes payable	$20
Total current liabilities	$50
Long-term loans	$30
Total Liabilities	$80
Common equity	$70
Total liabilities and equity	$150

Sales during the year were $100 million and are expected to grow by 50% in 2011. The fixed assets utilization in 2010 was 85%. Assume that the company's profit margin remains at 5% and the dividend payout ratio is 60%. Calculate the additional funds needed (AFN) in 2011.

8.2 XXX Inc. reported the following income statement for 2010 (in millions of dollars):

Income statement for 2010

Sales	$7,000
Operating expenses	$3,000
Operating profit (EBIT)	$4,000
Interest expense	$200
Profit before Tax (PBT)	$3,800
Taxes (@40%)	$1,520
Net Income	$2,280

The company's sales are expected to increase by 10% in 2011 and its operating costs will increase in proportion to sales. The interest expense is expected to remain the same and so will the tax rate. The dividend payout ratio will be 50%. What is the forecast addition to retained earnings in 2011?

8.3 ZZZ Inc. has the following balance sheet for 2010:

Balance sheet for 2010	(in million of dollars)
Assets	
Cash and cash equivalents	$5
Accounts receivable	$25
Inventory	$60
Total current assets	$90
Net plant and equipment	$110
Total assets	$200
Liabilities & Stockholders' equity	
Accounts payable	$20
Accrued liabilities	$10
Notes payable	$20
Total current liabilities	$50
Long-term loans	$30
Total Liabilities	$80
Common stock	$40
Retained earnings	$80
Total liabilities and equity	$200

Sales in 2010 were $500 million and the net income was $50 million. The company paid a dividend of $20 million to its common stockholders. The company is operating at full capacity. The sales for 2011 are projected to increase by 30%. Use the AFN equation to calculate the need for raising additional external capital.

This page is intentionally left blank

Glossary

Additional Funds Needed (AFN) - the amount of money needed by the company to sustain its business activities.

Asset Management Ratios –these are those ratios that show how well a company is managing its assets – fixed assets, inventory, accounts receivable etc.

Asset Turnover Ratio –given by (Sales/Total Assets).

Basic Earning Power (BEP) –given by (EBIT/Total Assets).

Capital Asset Pricing Model (CAPM) –an approach of estimating cost of retained earnings. Given by ($k_s = k_{RF} + (k_M - k_{RF}) \times b_i$).

Cash Conversion Cycle (CCC) – the amount of time a dollar is tied up in current assets. Given by (Inventory Conversion Period + DSO – Payables Deferral Period).

Cash Flow Adequacy Ratio –this ratio tells us whether a company is able to generate enough cash to pay for all its investing activities. Given by (Cash from Operating Activities/Cash used in Investing Activities).

Cash Flow Ratios –these are those ratios that are calculated using cash flow values from the company's statement of cash flows

Cash Flow to Net Income Ratio – given by (Cash from Operating Activities/Net Income).

Cash Times Interest Earned Ratio – given by (Cash earned before Interest and Tax/Interest expense).

Common-size Financial Statements – financial statements in which all income statement items are shown as a percentage of sales and all balance sheet items are shown as a percentage of total assets.

Cost of Capital – cost incurred by a company to borrow money in any form – debt, common equity, preferred stock.

Cost of Debt – interest paid by the company when borrowing money as loans, commercial paper, deposits, and all other fixed-interest bearing instruments.

Cost of Preferred Stock – interest paid by the company to its preferred stockholders

Cost of Retained Earnings –returns expected by the company's common stockholders when the company ploughs back its profits into business (instead of distributing it as dividends)

Current Ratio – given by (Current Assets/Current Liabilities).

Days Sales Outstanding (DSO) – given by (Accounts Receivable/Sales per day).

Discounted Cash Flow (DCF) Approach – a method of calculating cost of retained earnings. Given by ($k_s = (D_1/P_0) + g$).

Debt Ratio – given by (Total Liabilities/Total Assets).

Debt-to-equity Ratio – given by (Total Liabilities/Stockholders' equity).

Discounted Payback Period – the amount of time taken for return of invested capital using a discounting rate (equal to the cost of capital).

Dividend Yield – dividend as a percentage of stock price.

Dividend Reinvestment Plan (DRIP) – a way of distributing profit to shareholders by buying new stocks for them

DuPont Framework – a framework that breaks down return on equity (ROE) into Profitability, Efficiency and Leverage.

Ex-dividend Date - the date from which the dividend does not go with the stock.

Free Cash Flow (FCF) - the cash that remains for distribution to all investors, stockholders and debtors, after the company has made all investments in fixed assets, and in additional working capital needed to run its operations.

Flotation Cost – cost incurred by a company when issuing new common stock.

G ross Working Capital –is equal to the current assets of a company.

H amada Equation – a mathematical formula used to calculate the Beta value for a company. It is given by (b = b_u x [1 + (1 – T) x (D/E)]).

Holder-of-record Date – the date that occurs 2 working days after ex-dividend date. This is the date when the actual stock ownership is changed in the company's records.

I nventory Conversion Period –amount of time taken to convert inventory into finished goods.

Inventory Turnover Ratio – given by (Sales/Inventory).

Internal Rate of Return (IRR) – percentage of return given by an investment per year.

L everage Ratios – ratios that show how much debt a company is borrowing.

Liquidity Ratios – ratios that determine a company's liquidity position (current assets and liabilities).

M arket/Book (M/B) Ratio – given by (Market Price per share/Book value per share).

Market Value Ratios – ratios that compare a company's stock price with other values.

Modified IRR (MIRR) –a form of IRR that uses terminal values to calculate the returns on an investment. It removes some drawbacks with IRR.

N **et Operating Working Capital** – given by (Current assets – Non-interest bearing current liabilities).

Net Working Capital – given by (Current assets – current liabilities).

Net Operating Profit After Tax (NOPAT) –given by (EBIT x (1 – T)).

Net Present Value (NPV) –it is the current value of future cash flows.

P **rice/Earnings (P/E) Ratio** –given by (Market Price per share/Earnings per share).

Payables Deferral Period – amount of time available to pay off for purchases made by a company (the credit period).

Payback Period – amount of time taken to recover the investment made.

Pro forma –forecasted financial statements.

Profitability Ratios – ratios that show how profitable the company is in doing business.

Q **uick Ratio** – given by ((Current Assets – Inventories)/Current Liabilities).

Ratio Analysis – a tool used to analyze financial statements by calculating ratios.

Return On Assets (ROA) –given by (Net Income/Total Assets).

Return On Equity (ROE) – given by (Net Income/Stockholders' Equity).

Return On Sales (ROS) – given by (Net Income/Sales).

Spontaneous Liabilities – those liabilities that automatically change with the level of sales.

Stock Dividends – the practice of giving out additional stock as dividend instead of cash dividends.

Stock Splits –the practice of splitting a single stock into multiple stocks.

Times Interest Earned (TIE) Ratio – given by (EBIT/Interest expense).

Trade Credit – the credit available to a company on its purchases.

Weighted Average Cost of Capital (WACC) – the total cost of borrowings of a company, considering debt, common equity, and preferred stock.

Made in the USA
Lexington, KY
12 December 2019